'This powerful (in a goose bump kind of way), honest and practical book is a vital contribution as we navigate the Jesus journey into womanhood.'

Anne Calver, New Wine & Spring Harvest

'If I could prescribe this book to every Christian woman, I would. Rachel's warmth and wisdom shine from every page, and her deep well of experience combined with thought-provoking stories and helpful prompts for reflection left me feeling challenged, inspired and shouting "Amen!" at regular intervals. This book brilliantly and honestly articulates so much of what needs to be said about being a Christ-centred woman today. You can expect to have your mind renewed, your heart re-constructed and your passion reignited for cheering others on towards God's great purposes.'

Cathy Madavan, speaker, coach and author of
Digging for Diamonds and *Living On Purpose*

'This book is simply stunning; quite frankly, I couldn't put it down. I laughed and I cried as I read and explored the areas of life that we grapple with on a daily basis as young women. Rachel does an exceptional job of delving into the areas of body, mind, soul and strength with truth and honesty. I needed this book and am so grateful for it.'

Grace Wheeler, Youth For Christ National Evangelist

'I laughed and cried as I read this important book. Rachel is encouraging, biblical, practical and has an infectious passion for us all to live lives that are honest, free and full. This book is a great place to start.'

Abby Guinness, Head of Spring Harvest Programme, author and speaker

'Reading Rachel's book is like chatting with your best friend – funny, familiar, and sometimes just what you need to hear! Practical and full of truth from cover to cover.'

Charlotte Hendy, leader of The Esther Collective, an initiative from Girls' Brigade Ministries

'This book reads like a tender love letter, a powerful affirmation and a searing manifesto all at once – to women everywhere! Rachel helps us learn to deconstruct and dispose of the beliefs that have minimised, oppressed and captured us. Then she invites us to discover again the women that God created us to be in all our wild, unique, diverse wonder – and live courageously in the freedom that only Jesus can bring.'

Jo Saxton, speaker and author of *The Dream of You*

The Girl
De-Construction
Project

*Wildness, wonder and
being a woman*

RACHEL GARDNER

HODDER &
STOUGHTON

First published in Great Britain in 2018 by Hodder & Stoughton
An Hachette UK company

1

A CIP catalogue record for this title is available from the British Library

ISBN 978 1 473 68638 0
eBook ISBN 978 1 473 68639 7

Typeset in Sabon MT by Palimpsest Book Production Ltd, Falkirk, Stirlingshire
Printed and bound in the UK by CPI Group (UK) Ltd, Croydon CR0 4YY

Hodder & Stoughton policy is to use papers that are natural, renewable and recyclable
products and made from wood grown in sustainable forests. The logging and manufacturing
processes are expected to conform to the environmental regulations of the country of origin.

Hodder & Stoughton Ltd
Carmelite House
50 Victoria Embankment
London EC4Y 0DZ

www.hodderfaith.com

This book is lovingly dedicated to the luminous girls I grew up with – Taryn, Tammy, Sally and Zoe.

We didn't know then that we were helping to build each other into mighty women.

Maybe that's a good thing.

I think the knowledge would have blown our minds!

Rachel x

Contents

0.

DE-CONSTRUCT

I've tried to picture you as I write this book.

You're probably funnier than you think you are.

And stronger.

I imagine you have a piece of clothing in your wardrobe (or on your bedroom floor) that your friends roll their eyes at, but you absolutely love. I picture you standing just outside a door, taking a deep breath, wondering if you're confident enough to step inside. I think there are probably times when you feel sure of yourself. Your eyes light up and for a moment you're lost in your dreams. But then comes the uncertainty. You second-guess yourself. A cloud passes across your face and for a moment you're lost in self-doubt.

You're probably a little taller, or shorter, than you'd like to be. You're too old to be labelled a girl, but don't sit easy with 'woman' just yet. But that's exactly who you are. A phenomenal woman. You might be a woman of colour, a woman of passion, a woman with freckles, a woman with a story.

Maybe I'm right. Maybe I'm not. But one thing I'm certain of is that you're uniquely and wonderfully you.

I also know that *who* you are begins with God. He is the reference point for all of life. *Nothing* makes sense without him. *Nothing* good and lasting is ours outside of him. As you find yourself in him, you expand in faith, hope and love. You find your feet as a woman.

Maybe I'm getting a bit ahead of myself. So let me tell you something about me.

Like you, I'm stronger than I think I am. Sometimes funnier too.

I mostly learn the important things by making mistakes. I'm eager for meaningful connection with people. Sometimes this feels good. Other times I feel propelled into behaviours I know aren't healthy but numb my fear that I don't belong. I love God. I want to love him more. I'm convinced that Jesus is the promise of hope for every area of my life. Even on the days when I doubt I'm loved. Even on the days when I wonder if God is here.

I try hard not to judge myself for the insecurities and hypocrisies that undermine my desire to live for Jesus. But I'm discovering that the only way to live fear-free is to choose to belong to God. To live in ways that make no sense if Jesus isn't walking with me.

This is what I long for.

In writing this book I've spent a bit of time in my past. I've dug out old diaries (pre social media days!) and called up old friends, curious to discover what we were like as teenagers and what kind of women we hoped to become.

My teenage friends and I were the generation entering independence on the brink of the digital sexual revolution. Young, eager to please and naïve, we didn't understand our yearnings. We flailed about, sometimes crashing into each other, sometimes hiding ourselves away. Always comparing and finding ourselves wanting. Always going to the loo en masse. Always dreaming that something better was just around the corner.

Our brushes with boys, drugs, alcohol, ouija boards, self-harm and romance felt like signs that we were either winning or losing in this game where no one knew what got you 'in' but everyone knew when you were 'out'. Train-track braces and A-line school skirts added insult to injury as we found it increasingly difficult to reconcile the ordinary female bodies we had with the dazzling ones we saw in the media. The seeds of self-loathing had already been sown.

The one thing we all craved was the one thing we couldn't really articulate: confidence. So we oriented ourselves around the Girls-Who-Didn't-Care. Teachers and students seemed to part like waves when these goddesses walked the school corridor. Oozing disdain and secret knowledge, they had *it*. So we scuttled around after them, hoping that if we could just get proximate to these other-worldly beings, their certainty would rub off on us. Of course, it took years before any of us realised that we were all playing at this thing called 'girl'. Some of us were just better actors than others.

At the exact same time that our culture was carefully cultivating our dislike of ourselves, we were also discovering a radical alternative narrative: Christianity's story of surrender. From pulpits and festival stages, we heard again and again about how losing ourselves was actually the only path to finding ourselves. Already being losers meant that this didn't feel like too much of an ask. So we jumped in. We set up the school Christian union and prayed for revival. Loads of girls came (it was an all-girl school). Possibly because we provided crisps and the sexy youth worker from the local church. But he told us about Jesus. This God-guy who we experienced as part Superman, part boyfriend. And although our faith may have been driven by our intense emotional reactions, it was still genuine. What we were discovering was breathing hope into our young hearts that we could live lives that mattered.

What we were discovering was also throwing up questions about who we were going to be for the rest of our lives. Celebrity culture said one thing. Church another. Whose girl were we going to be? Couldn't we just be free and belong to ourselves? Surely you can only lose yourself to Jesus if you know you are yours to give in the first place? In a messy but important way, the girl de-construction project was beginning.

In the years since, I've listened to thousands of women of all ages, expressing the same longing to know who they are but getting stuck in chasing opinions they are told count more than God's. Mostly these women, like me, have won the lottery of being born into the affluent West. Many have grown up in a Christian faith community. But not all. And not all who have had the material stuff of life sorted have found life easy or knowing who they are straightforward. Whatever their background, what each woman craves is to live free from fake, free from fear and free to pursue the life God has for them.

Is this what you long for as well?

Whatever age you are, you're on the path of becoming *you*, whether or not it's the 'you' you could be, or the 'you' you think you should settle for. You may be feeling fully aware of who you are and confident about who you're becoming. You may be asking the deepest of questions that leave you wondering who you'll be tomorrow let alone in the distant future. You may be somewhere between the two.

It's OK. Not because knowing who you are isn't important. But because knowing who you are doesn't start with you; it starts with the God who created you and is more attentive to you and who you're becoming than you could possibly imagine. This can make you bold as you embrace your life and seek to live it well!

> 'Can a mother forget the infant at her breast,
> walk away from the baby she bore?
> But even if mothers forget,
> I'd never forget you – never.
> Look, I've written your names on the backs of my hands.
> The walls you're rebuilding are never out of my sight.'
>
> Isaiah 49:15–16, *The Message*

If you're willing and able, please fold your arms.

How was that? Easy I guess. You do it all the time, mostly without thinking. It's like second nature.

Now fold them the opposite way.

That's more difficult because I'm asking you to unlearn what you normally do without thinking. I'm asking you to pay attention to what goes unnoticed and then find the opposite way. No one sat you down when you were three and told you, 'In our family we fold our arms *this* way.' You just picked it up. Why not? It's how we discover most things. They're caught, not taught.

But what if we catch something that isn't good, or right? What if, along the way, we've picked up ideas about what it means to be a Christian woman that just aren't working? What if we're tangled up in beliefs about who we should or could be that might be holding us back from finding our feet as the women God has made us to be?

This book is my invitation to you to do some de-construction. Part manifesto, part women's stories, it's an encouragement to ask questions and make changes to enable you to experience not only your belovedness, but also your power as a woman. To help you explore your identity in ways that you can define and redefine as you daily ally yourself to Christ.

It's been written in the gaps in my life between youth work, parenting, prepping for talks, hanging out with friends, singing at the top of my voice, loving my neighbour, cleaning my car and cooking dinner. But in my experience, the best things happen in those in-between moments. Wild things grow in gaps.

The book is separated into four sections to try and cover the areas I feel we need to dig into.

Body

Your body is breathtaking, both in beauty and significance in God's dream for your life and calling. These chapters will help you gain a more intimate knowledge of your body's desires and will empower you to take control in how you live, lead and love with and through your body.

Mind

God made you to be a thinking woman with a brilliant mind that can solve problems and create new ways of doing things. These chapters will encourage you to see how your thoughts don't need to dictate the direction of your life. You can choose to chase after all that is good, true, pure, praiseworthy and life-bringing.

Soul

A time to explore more of your inner life as you expand into the mystery of God. These chapters will inspire you to choose soulful connections, helping you build a life you don't need to escape from. When you pause to experience rest with God, the adventure can begin.

Strength

You are courageous at heart as you walk the path of self-surrender, not self-obliteration. These chapters will help you to break free from female cultural ideas that don't fit you and don't glorify Jesus. As you bring your power under the authority of Christ, you will know more joy and strength of purpose.

At the end of each chapter there are some questions to help you tune in to what God may be saying specifically to you. Knowledge gives us the ability to take things apart. That's what I hope these chapters enable you to do. To take apart some of the lies and false hopes that have left you disappointed with yourself, the church, wider culture and God. But I don't plan to leave you there! You're in the hands of a loving God who has a future and a hope for you. So I also share wisdom to help you put your hopes, dreams and expectations together in new ways. I hope that you will trust God to put you on your feet as the woman he has made you to be.

'*De*-construct me' invites you to do something personal about the questions the chapter has raised for you. This is not an opportunity to shame yourself, but to understand yourself more fully. The question(s) might inspire you to challenge a long-held belief or to look deeper into a habit or choice to consider whether it's right for you or compatible with your identity in Christ.

'*Re*-construct me' invites you to participate in who you're becoming. The question(s) might inspire you to pick up a new habit, or define a new way of thinking or acting. Mostly, it's an opportunity to draw your whole being in line with the powerful work God will be doing in your life as you invite him to build you in love (see Ephesians 3:16–18).

I hope that as you journey through this book you'll know how much God delights in you. The Bible tells us that he rejoices over us with singing. Imagine that. The greatest voice in the entire universe singing love songs over you! You're not yet the finished work of art. Your life is a book still being written. You're a song that has yet to reach the bridge. The best is still yet to come.

Yours in the beautiful process of being built in the likeness of Jesus,

Wild & Wonderful,
Rachel x

'. . . take a firm stand, feet on the ground and head high. Keep a tight grip on what you were taught, whether in personal conversation or by our letter. May Jesus himself and God our Father, who reached out in love and surprised you with gifts of unending help and confidence, put a fresh heart in you, invigorate your work, enliven your speech.'

2 Thessalonians 2:16–17, *The Message*

BODY.

'The first problem for all of us . . . is not to learn, but to unlearn.'

Gloria Steinem

'Before I shaped you in the womb,
   I knew all about you.
Before you saw the light of day,
   I had holy plans for you . . .'
                              Jeremiah 1:5, *The Message*

I

NUDE

'Your naked body should only belong to those who fall in love with your naked soul.'

Charlie Chaplin

I undressed and stared hard at myself in the mirror.

At fifteen I was already an old hand at this. It didn't take long to reel off the litany of disasters I saw before me: spotty face, wonky smile, bow legs, no boobs. I don't remember when exactly I started to see my body as a project. But somewhere between learning to walk and having my first period, I had taken the hint that it wasn't enough to have a body that worked. I would have to have my body worked on. I swung between that dreamy adolescent state of being convinced that my prince would come, and the harsh reality that if my prince was on his way, he would definitely choose my best friend over me. I sucked in my cheeks and tilted my head at funny angles to get the light splashing onto the 'right' features – anything to make me look better, more beautiful, more like 'them' or 'her' or 'me' or whoever the hell I was supposed to be.

I sighed.

It was no good. I just didn't have *it*.

My friend had lent me some of her clothes. Grabbing them off the floor I caught the whiff of teenage desperation and powdery body spray. They felt like someone else's skin. They felt hard boiled and dangerous. I put them on. I wanted to be splendid, gorgeous and desirable. For boys to want to get with me and girls to want to be me. Isn't that how it's meant to work, how I'm meant to feel? How girls are supposed to be?

But I just felt uncomfortable.

How do I do this whole girl thing? I pleaded with my reflection. Screwing my eyes shut tight, I imagined opening them and all this devastating discomfort would disappear. I imagined looking like girls on the telly and in magazines: outstanding, totally nailing it all the flipping time. Helplessly, effortlessly stunning.

And airbrushed.

I learnt along the way that most images in magazines are digitally manipulated to look a certain way, but back then fake felt real whereas my real felt incompetent and shameful. And that's how I felt for many years. These were the days before social media and selfies. But we didn't need internet technology to tell us that female beauty has a price tag. Sadly some of us were already cutting or starving ourselves to deal with the pain and shame of not feeling good enough.

I guess you may have a similar story. Years of squeezing into such a narrow ideal of beauty can leave us feeling misshapen and objectified. We live in a world where advertising uses women's semi-naked Photoshopped bodies as objects to sell everything. When society objectifies a person it's taken the first step towards justifying all sorts of offensive and violent behaviour against that person. Aggressive objectification plays out both in women's lives and in society as a whole.

No more nudes?

Many of us struggle to accept our bodies. We fear the ridicule and rejection of letting people see us just as we are. So we either max up the glamour dial until we can't recognise ourselves any more, or we choose invisibility. Both come from the same core belief: 'There's something about me that's lacking, and everyone can see it.'

Recently I found myself in the media debating female nudity. I was being labelled a prude and misogynist for suggesting that society should not encourage teenage girls to send nude selfies. As a passionate advocate for empowering girls and women I was incensed by the lie that circulating images of your breasts and vagina online is inherently liberating.

I had campaigned with my friend Rebecca Rumsey against a fashion house that had chosen to display in pink neon the words 'Send Me Nudes' on the back wall of their flagship store. As their target audience is teenage girls we asked them why they were asking underage girls to expose their naked bodies for anyone who asked for it. For a brand all about female empowerment, they had just reinforced to a generation of young women the lie that the only thing about them that matters is their exposed and highly sexualised bodies.

Could you imagine a similar slogan on the wall of a

fashion store that serves young men? Of course not, because in our culture a boy's worth is seen in his ability to use his body, not display it.

The 'Send Me Nudes' campaign caught people's imagination and after three days there was so much pressure on this fashion house that the neon sign came down. But the fight over the misuse of women's bodies continues. The existence of phrases like 'Rape Culture' (meaning an environment where misogynist attitudes normalise and trivialise sexual assault and abuse of girls and women) shines a light on the deep fault in our society. Rape isn't about sex, it's about control and power over someone's body. The phenomenon of boys demanding nudes from girls exists in a culture where men see it as their right to possess women's bodies.

It's one of the saddest parts of my work with young teenage girls – the impact that all these years of their bodies being subjected to the scrutiny of the online world will invariably have on how they see themselves. And many of the young girls I support are completely oblivious to it.

Nude love

But even with someone we love and feel safe with, we might pull back, feeling awkward under their gaze. Chloe told me she sometimes can't handle her boyfriend looking closely at her: 'I hate the thought he can see my spots and hairy bits round my hairline. It's gross. I know it sounds weird but it really freaks me out that he can see that much.'

Isn't this where our cultural obsession with filters comes from? The fear that our natural beauty is lacking, that pretence is more beautiful than authenticity. We find ourselves feeding off each other's lies and then believing we're alone in our dislike or mistrust of our bodies.

The thing is, we all know it's fake. Beneath the concealer and filters we're just us. We've probably met people whose Instagram pictures look nothing like their real selves. Some of us might have fallen into that trap. So why do we find it so hard to resist or disrupt the culture of beauty that oppresses so many of us?

It's because of something called a fractured body schema. In essence this means that we don't see our bodies the same way that other people see them. It's like we're constantly looking at ourselves in a smashed mirror, trying to put all these isolated bits together to make a complete image. But it looks wrong. We struggle to see ourselves as we truly are.

You might not be fifteen any more, but if you're still battling a deep conviction that you don't fit the female body ideal, you're not alone. These bodies we wage war over have been given us by a loving creator God. They are the most incredible vessels with which to experience the world around us. If we didn't have bodies, we wouldn't be human. Dancing, soaking in a hot bath, bungee jumping, kissing, creating art or making a noise – none of this would be possible if we weren't made of skin and bone.

So where shall we begin in our act of resistance of the fake and the false?

By getting naked!

You were born nude. Everything about you needed the

loving care and attention of people in your life who stepped up to love and nurture you. 'Naked I came from my mother's womb, naked I'll return to the womb of the earth' (Job 1:21, *The Message*).

Your original state of nakedness is absolutely crucial to understanding God's design for your life; you are created to live free from pretence and disguise. I'm not talking about heading off to college or work with nothing but your handbag and brolly in case it rains! Goodness, how would anyone be able to get on with the mundane boring business of life after seeing you stunning and starkers at 9.00 a.m. on a Monday morning?

God's beautiful design for all humanity was that we wouldn't need to cover ourselves up for fear of people not being able to control their urges around us. The possibility that anyone would use your body to exploit or reject you was *never* part of the design. The idea of clothes full stop was not part of the original design. There was no need for them.

In the book of Genesis the first humans stood talking with God face to face and completely nude. It was the most natural and obvious way to be. There was no fear of rejection, so they felt nothing but utter wholeness in their nakedness. 'The two of them, the Man and his Wife, were naked, but they felt no shame' (Genesis 2:25, *The Message*). God only had to clothe Eve and Adam once they took him out of the picture. The moment they disobeyed God they set in motion a de-creation, where human selfishness took centre stage – and has been there ever since. When God was their reference point they could look at each other with complete innocence, knowing only self-giving love. Eve is the *only* woman in history to have had a time where she never needed to question how safe or accepted she was as she stood naked in the presence of a man. It's after she and Adam reject God's command that they feel the shame of being naked. Not because being naked is bad, but because a world where people put their own needs first is not a safe place to live a naked, undefended life.

The fear you may have that your body is not good enough to be loved stems from the sin that took root in the world way back at the start of time. But this doesn't have to be how you experience your body. You can live shame-free in your body. This starts with embracing the truth of who you are. So here it is.

God sees you exactly as you are. Which means that God sees your body. And this is what he says to you, right now, wherever you are:

> 'Behold, you are beautiful, my love;
> behold, you are beautiful;
> your eyes are doves.'
>
> Song of Solomon 1:15, ESV

In God's eyes you are beautiful as you are; unadorned, undisguised, unexaggerated, simply you. It's not just your growing character and surrendered heart that he delights in (although he does). He calls your physicality lovely. Remember that God is completely unlimited by culture and sin. He doesn't sexualise, criticise or compare. As my friend Rebecca says, 'From conception, God has covered you in your own standard of beauty and you exceed it every day.'

Maybe you're more comfortable with the idea of God seeing your naked soul than you are with God seeing your naked body. Millennia of being subjected to the male gaze can make it hard for women to experience being seen by another as a liberating experience. But knowing that God sees us completely and loves us unconditionally is the source of our hope and strength.

Here are some steps to help you move forward in your relationship with your body.

1. Know your body

Your body needs you to take the lead. This starts with a real awareness of your body: sight, sound, smell, sensation, appetite and experience.

You could start with your hands. Look closely at the skin on your palms and wrists, the marks on the back of your hands, the skin around your nails. Don't pass judgement on what you see. Just look at it. Then begin to allow your mind to wonder what your hands might need from you. More hand cream? A break from nail varnish for a while? To be held in someone else's hands? Let your mind think more broadly than just the obvious physical needs; what are your hands telling you about what you as a whole person might need?

- To stop biting them, because you want to stop destroying a part of your body.
- To hold them out to God, because you need to let go of something that's been weighing heavily on your heart.

- To give yourself a manicure, because you're in need of demonstrating kindness and care to yourself.
- To build or bake something because your creativity hasn't found positive expression for a while.

You could do the same exercise with other parts of your body, too. How are your eyes feeling – tired? strained? What might this be telling you about what you need – to get to bed earlier or give yourself a break from screens for an hour, or an evening? Getting to know our bodies can help us understand what we might need, which helps us take control of responding positively to those needs. At times our physical needs can feel overwhelming, to the point of hijacking our freedom to choose healthily. What can help us to feel more control over how we respond to our needs is discovering what our body is telling us. How does being hungry affect you? Or feeling angry? When you experience stress and anxiety how is that felt in your body?

I know my body well enough now to spot when hunger is taking me into the grumpy zone. Even as an adult, I have an inclination to expect other people to sort out what I'm going to eat! Not taking responsibility for getting enough sleep is another way that we can act irresponsibly with the bodies we've been given. Eating and sleeping enough are crucial to our well-being and the well-being of people around us. There are times when I've asked God why life is so tough right now, only to become quickly aware that I can do something positive to help deal with the situation by eating regularly and going to bed earlier. Loving God with all of our body means sometimes fighting with the strength of our bodies that God provides.

In the first book of Kings we read about Elijah, who slaughters the prophets of the most powerful queen of the day, Jezebel. She is a terrifying force to be reckoned with and on hearing that she's out to murder him, Elijah runs away. But you can only run for so long. Exhausted, he collapses under a bush in the Judean desert and begs God to let him die.

'"I have had enough, LORD," he prayed. "Let me die. I am no better than my ancestors." Then he lay down under the tree and slept. Suddenly an angel came to him and touched him. "Get up and eat," the angel said. Elijah saw near his head a loaf baked over coals and a jar of water, so he ate and drank. Then he went back to sleep. Later the LORD's angel came to him a second time. The angel touched him and said, "Get up and eat. If you don't, the journey will be too hard for you." So Elijah got up and ate and drank. The food made him strong enough to walk for forty days and nights to Mount Sinai, the mountain of God.'

1 Kings 19:4–8, NCV

When he gets to Mount Sinai God sends fire and wind to break open huge rocks and shake the ground. After this comes the gentlest wind, which blows around Elijah's body. In that moment Elijah covers his face knowing that God is close. He *feels* God on his skin. In making Elijah eat and sleep, God was strengthening Elijah's body to recognise him when he felt him. Our bodies matter because they are the place where we are able to experience God.

Have you ever sensed God with your body? It might have been in a church service or when you were running home in the rain, but you felt something *more* in your body than you would ordinarily feel. You might describe it as the invisible presence of a loving being. I try to feel God through my senses of touch, sight, sound and taste. If it's raining I might lift my face and imagine that God is gently touching me with each raindrop.

Here are some other questions to help you know your body:

1. What parts of my body are a mystery to me?

2. What hurts right now?

3. What scars and wounds do I carry on my body?

4. When do I feel 'out of my body' or disconnected from my body?

5. When do I sense God on or in my body?

6. What physical experiences make me feel distant from God? Is this true? What might I do to remind myself of God's powerful presence, within and around me?

7. Are there any needs that I neglect or over-indulge?

8. When I next look at myself naked, what truth will I speak over myself? 'This is my body. God created my whole body. God loves all of me.'

2. Love your body

Loving your body is simply choosing to look at your body with the eyes of love. If you're going to invite God to build you into the woman he desires you to be, do it out of love, not fear. Anything done without love comes to nothing.

In one of the most popular parts of the Bible read out at weddings, Paul defines love along the lines of God's character: faithful, kind, giving, protective. How can these characteristics define how you show love to your body? Take a look at the list I've taken from 1 Corinthians 13 and maybe jot down one practical thing you could do to take seriously the call to love your body.

- I will be patient with my body by . . .

- I will be kind to my body by . . .

- Instead of comparing my body to others, I will . . .

- Instead of flaunting my body, I will . . .

- I will be open with my body by . . .

- I will be honest about my body by . . .

Loving your body is about embracing your flaws, both visible and invisible. It means looking in a mirror and choosing to see the truth about our bodies. There are some mirrors I love because they flatter me (the ones in dimly lit wine bars are great) and mirrors I hate because they floor me (every mirror in a shop changing room!). But I don't need to be flattered and I don't deserve to be floored. What I need is to have the courage to see myself as clearly as I am able, and then ask God to help me to accept and even love myself for it.

We need the help of the Holy Spirit for this because what we're talking about is a deep and unshakable knowledge of our belovedness. It's so easy to experience our bodies as unlovely and unloved. We might not even realise we're doing it! But when we do this we hold ourselves back from those we love, fearing that they think we're unlovely too. This couldn't be further from the truth. The enemy of your soul is also the enemy of your body. He hates the good work that God has done in creating you and the good work that Christ is doing within you – so he will do all that is in his limited power to undermine your ability to love your body.

When I discovered that I was unable to naturally conceive children, I felt like a stranger in my own body. It felt like a broken vessel that was getting in the way of my long held dream of being a mother. I hated my dead womb and redundant ovaries. And don't get me started on the pointlessness of my periods! I was so sad and so angry at God and at my body. For a while sex with my husband felt pointless too. Then I came to the realisation that I was rejecting the very body that Christ had given his life for and my husband had covenanted his life to. I'm more than just my body, but I am certainly not me without it. The turning point in my healing wasn't conceiving a baby; that still hasn't happened. The healing came as I began embracing my imperfections and choosing to *love* my body and love *with* my body.

You and I can absolutely claim these words over our broken and beautiful bodies:

'You made my whole being;
    you formed me in my mother's body.
I praise you because you made me in an amazing and wonderful way.
    What you have done is wonderful.
    I know this very well.'

Psalm 139:13–14, NCV

3. Own your body

'Shout out to all the women, across the world, using their brains, their strength, their work ethic, their talent, their "magic" that they were born with, that only they possess. It may never bring you as much "attention" or bank notes as using your body, but women like you don't need that kind of "attention". In the quiet moments, you will feel something deeper than fleeting excitement resulting from attention; you will feel something called pride and respect. Keep on resisting the urge to cave. You'll never have to make silly excuses for yourself.'

P!nk

We often talk about having a vision for our life (family, career, calling and so on) but how about having a vision for your body? You are not a disembodied spirit outside of yourself and looking in. You are em-bodied, which means you have the God-given right and responsibility to make choices over what you eat, wear, do and feel.

Although we may feel the victims of circumstance and experiences that are beyond our control the truth is that we are able to choose from this moment how we will live in these bodies God has given us.

A fierce debate rages around women's right to take control over their bodies. It plays out in conversations around reproductive rights, abortion, sexual consent, pornography, the male gaze in films and so on. The Christian community isn't immune. The problem is decades of the subordination of women's bodies to male ownership where men make the decisions *for* women and *about* women. This can happen in marriages as much as it can happen in churches, offices, friendship groups and nations.

The Bible has a very different take on body ownership which in a nutshell is that we are all responsible for our own choices. Even in marriage, the woman and man both offer their bodies to each other in mutual submission. There's no suggestion of controlling each other in Paul's instructions to the new Christians in Corinth.

'The husband should give his wife all that he owes her as his wife. And the wife should give her husband all that she owes him as her husband. The wife does not have full rights over her own body; her husband shares them. And the husband does not have full rights over his own body; his wife shares them. Do not refuse to give your bodies to each other, unless you both agree to stay away from sexual relations for a time so you can give your time to prayer. Then come together again so Satan cannot tempt you because of a lack of self-control.'

1 Corinthians 7:3–5, NCV

One of the evidences of the Holy Spirit being at work in someone's life is that they demonstrate greater self-control over their bodies. But in Scripture, control over your body is always understood as the freedom to surrender control to God. My decisions over what I do with and to my body are mine to make in the power of the Spirit and in line with what I understand to be God's desires for my life. I am responsible for my own actions and am open to challenge from others who feel constrained or offended by my choices. All too often I come across women who have been *told* to cover up because it's leading men astray.

This comes back to the lack of self-control again. Women shouldn't be covering up *so that* men don't have to deal with their lustful thoughts. Men (and women) should take control over their lustful thoughts. But equally it is immature for us not to consider the impact of choices on people around us. I'm not exercising self-control if I knowingly behave in such a way that makes life difficult for someone else.

Godly control over my body begins with acknowledging that it is *my* body! This enables me to exercise the capacity I have to make good, godly decisions. It includes the following actions:

- speaking up about inappropriate behaviour another person has shown towards me
- eating a balanced diet
- having personal boundaries around how my image is presented online
- dressing in ways that express my whole self, not to impress a small minority of people

- not apologising for being myself
- physically reaching out to others in need of comfort and care

4. Surrender your body

My Christian life is at the expense of Christ's life. I can never pay him back. But what I can do is use my body in ways that honour him.

It's not that I don't care about my body any more; in fact, I value my body *more*. If my body is the place where I experience the presence of God, I don't want to hurt the place he has made his home. If my body is the place I reach out to the world with God's love, I don't want to contradict the one I'm living for. I don't want to damage it. Not because I think I'm all that great, but because he is! Whether that's a tattoo, outfit, decision about sexual behaviour or eating plan, my body needs to tell the truth about God.

This is what Paul means when he says our bodies are made for the true worship of God. 'I plead with you to give your bodies to God because of all he has done for you. Let them be a living and holy sacrifice—the kind he will find acceptable. This is truly the way to worship him' (Romans 12:1, NLT).

God invites us to live naked before him. Mask-free. Undisguised. Honest. Not dressed in the lies of pretence or in our best achievements, but just as we are. With nothing left to offer except our very selves. The miracle is that we are fully embraced in our nakedness and clothed with love and power as the children of God.

And yet, I wonder if there are moments when God chooses to see us only to the extent that we let him. He sees and knows everything, but does he hang back, eager for us to trust him enough with our undefended self? I remember having a disagreement with my husband. It was as we were getting ready for bed. I suddenly became aware that I was half undressed. And in that moment of feeling vulnerable I grabbed my shirt to cover myself up. Our unkind words to each other had a direct impact on my capacity to stand naked before the man I love with all my heart.

God knows your fear of vulnerability. It might be that rejection from others makes you fear God's rejection of you too. But God will never reject you. Being naked before God is acknowledging that nothing hides us from him. We can try to fill the space between him and us. We can try to make ourselves more worthy of his love. But none of this works. In the end all we can do is surrender ourselves to the God who sees and loves us as we are. He makes it possible for us to see and love ourselves as we are. He makes it possible for us to live boldly in our bodies.

Here's my prayer for living free and bold in my body. Why not make it your prayer too?

Beautiful Creator, my desire is that I will . . .
look at my body with love
make good choices for my body
listen well to my body's desires
give my body to the one I have covenanted my life to
love my body for what it allows me to give and experience
choose to be seen but not mistake this for being loved.

Protect me from the toxicity of . . .
shaming my own or other people's bodies
obsessively perfecting or pretending to be who I'm not
fearing my body changing as I get older
using my body to gain influence.

Draw my attention to the times when the way I handle my
    body's needs distracts me from you.
Wake me up to the many ways I can experience you
    in my body.
Amen.

De-construct me

How do you feel about your body? We spend so much time choosing the clothes we cover our bodies with that we forget we have a body that we can choose to love and care for. Have you ever stood in front of a mirror naked? How was that? What words came into your mind about what you saw in the mirror? You might want to try it and see the way you 'other' yourself. I would say that any critical label you give yourself is you 'othering' yourself – viewing yourself as a project in need of work instead of the precious and beautiful woman you already are.

Here are some of the labels I've 'othered' myself with over the years:

'Frumpy and boring.'

'What is *that* all about?!'

'Too flabby, too flat chested, too hairy, too pear-shaped.'

'No one will ever get excited about that.'

I would *never* say any of these things to anyone else, but somehow I've thought it OK to say them to myself. But that can change – you and I are unique in our physical beauty, and we have the power to accept our bodies *as they are*.

Re-construct me

I'd love to challenge you to speak truth over your body for a week. How about this? – 'My body is breathtaking both in beauty and significance in God's dream for my life and his mission.' If that doesn't feel like something you'd say, rewrite it. I know someone who looks at herself in the mirror and says, 'Body – you're ready!' It's her kick back against the 'beach-body' adverts that tell women how to get a perfect body before they hit the beach. She's declaring that her body is life-ready!

You might also like to choose one way that you will demonstrate loving ownership of your body this week. Is there an unhealthy habit you want to challenge or a new habit you want to adopt? Watch that you don't shame yourself if you struggle to follow it through. Be kind to yourself and be proud of yourself each time you choose loving authority over your body.

2.

DESIRE

'Here I am back and still smouldering with passion, like a wine smoking. Not a passion any longer for flesh, but a complete hunger for you. A devouring hunger.'

Henry Miller to lover Anaïs Nin, in *Nearer the Moon*[1]

I remember, in my mid teens, stumbling across an erotic diary. *Nearer the Moon*, by Anaïs Nin, to be exact. Every time I opened the book it was as if white heat was pouring from the page. It was scandalous and exciting – nothing like the reproductive stuff I knew from textbooks. Then years later I read *Lady Chatterley's Lover*. I found it one grey afternoon in the school library, a lust-story set in the 1930s and banned in the UK for many years for its 'obscene' content. In brief it tells the story of a high society woman stuck in a sexless marriage who has an affair with her husband's rough-but-ready game keeper, in a shed. The main thing I took away from reading it was that naming genitalia is actually a thing.

But a penis-name aside, these books were introducing me to sex in a way I had never heard it talked about in church. For all I thought I knew about the business of sex, I had no idea about *this*. I'm sure people in my church probably *did* talk about sex, but never about enjoying it or understanding the urges and desires that accompanied it.

And so began years of wondering about everything I had read. What would it feel like to touch or be touched? How would I know that I was with the right man? If sex was off limits before marriage, was masturbation allowed? What about the night-time sex dreams I had no control over? Or the day-dream fantasies that I did? But I didn't know who to ask, or how to ask my questions – so I didn't. Instead I tried to be a good Christian girl and resist the 'wrong' sort of things, but it was in a muted way. I rarely put into words what I was thinking or what I wanted.

One night at a school friend's party I was confronted with a guy responding to my supposed 'bedroom eyes'. My what? I can't even remember if I did actually look at him. I might have looked in his general vicinity, but not to call him over on the promise of sex! I was baffled.

Then there was the guy at a Christian conference centre who told his friends he daren't be alone in a room with me if I continued to touch his arm when I talked to him. I was sixteen. I remember feeling confused about who he was afraid of, himself or me?

But I didn't say anything.

Now I'd have something to say to both guys. First, if you think a woman looking in your direction is sexual consent, or being alone with a teenage girl will put you at risk of doing something against your will, then it's probably time to hand yourself in at the local police station.

But that was then and this is now. Of course I know

countless men who would never think or act like this. And I'm not wanting to be negative about these young guys themselves. They were probably just acting out attitudes they had been told to believe were OK. But I want to be very negative about the culture of silence that surrounds sexual desire and wrongly elevates a false righteousness. Not talking about sex isn't being holy; it's being dangerous because it can lead us to believe all kinds of unhelpful or even damaging things about God's gift of sexual desire. Blaming other people for your inability to control yourself sexually isn't being a good Christian, it's being an unsafe person.

Throughout my teens I *never* asked anything about my sexual curiosities, and I never *did* anything either. People thought I was a bastion of purity. I was mainly a highly risk-averse teenager!

There are so many myths about female sexual desire.

Freud referred to female sexuality as the 'dark continent', meaning it's something that's dangerous to navigate and impossible to understand. It's highly likely that this was because all study of human sexuality up until that time had been focused on men's sexual desires and genitalia. But this fact alone means that there has been so much damage done in society and the church when it comes to preconceptions about women and our sexual desires.

In church history we stumble across a whole plethora of theological giants who knew real confusion when it came to understanding sexuality. 'What is the difference whether it is in a wife or a mother?' asked St Augustine. 'It is still Eve the tempter that we must beware of in any woman. I fail to see what use woman can be to man, if one excludes the function of bearing children.'[2] Whether their own sexual inadequacies have always been at play or not, it's clear that for generations a misreading of the book of Genesis, casting Eve as the ultimate sexual temptress, has done much to make female sexuality a deeply worrying thing.

As Christian women, we don't always have an easy relationship with the fact that we're sexual beings with genitalia, reproductive organs, sexual appetites and thoughts, experiences and goals. There's a whole pile of self-regulating repressive behaviour that happens in many of us that derives from deep confusion and fear about getting it wrong and being shamed. I get that. It's difficult to reconcile our immense capacity for sexual desire with our longing to be godly. They can feel like different goals.

But if there's one word that offers a way forward, it's this – purity.

Often misunderstood, sometimes weaponised, purity is powerful. It's not about what you do or don't do, it's about *who you are* and how you choose to respond to your sexual desires.

You feel desire because God feels desire. His desire is for us, and ultimately our desire is for him. Sexual desire is essentially a sign deep within our beings that we're made to be one with God in intimate, lasting and satisfying relationship with him. In her book *God, Sexuality and the Self*, theologian Sarah Coakley puts it like this: 'There's a divine meaning to sexual desire. It's the precious clue that ever tugs at the heart, reminding the human soul – however dimly – of its created source.'[3]

But although our desires come from God, not all the

ways we experience or express our desires *honour* God. Just because we feel sexual desire for someone doesn't mean that having sex with them would please God or be the right use of our sexuality – for example, if I have sex with someone who is already married to someone else, or if I have sex with someone I'm not married to.

In these times, I need God's help both to help me not have sex with someone who's not mine to get between the sheets with, and to help me handle the strong sexual desires I have for them. I need both the strength to make good decisions, even in the heat of the moment, and a way to redirect my desires so that I'm not continually tempted to give in.

This is where purity comes in.

The starting point of sexual purity is having a pure desire for God, as in a totally devoted surrender to who he is and what he asks of us. When our desire for God is the greatest desire of our being, our sexual desire for others finds its best expression – pointing us towards God and helping us to see how even the most overwhelming desires don't need to control our actions. Increasingly this strengthens us to know we are free to choose what to do with our sexual desires.

This wonderful reorientation of our deep desires towards God doesn't happen overnight. It's a journey of discovering what it feels like to be sexual beings and where we're prone to chase what we want, rather than how God might want us to express our desires.

I remember hungering after a guy. My sexual desire for him felt like physical starvation. He was everything I wanted in a lover and he quickly became my great obsession. We dated for a while. We didn't have sex but we intensely explored each other's bodies. When the relationship ended I was left lonely, hurt and angry – and desperately wanted to feel better about myself. Masturbating felt like something I could do to take myself back to being with him. But the more I did it the more shame I felt. The sexual urges felt overwhelming and out of my control. I wasn't sleeping around or seeking a new relationship but I began to fear that I would never be free from just doing what my body craved.

When we make people the object of our obsessions we cease to see them as people in their own right with free will and choice; we just see them as a means to our happiness and fulfilment. We also cease to believe in our own capacity to heal and be whole without them. We become our own judge and jailor. Purity is a beam of light reminding us that all our desires are met in God and him alone.

One night I was lying in my bed, crying my eyes out over the mess I was making of my relationships and sexuality. I felt broken and full of temptation to satisfy my sexual urges. I got off the bed and knelt on the floor, crunched up and crying out to God. I don't remember what I prayed. But God knew my heart and my longing – and he found me. It felt as though someone was hugging me as I knelt on the floor. I was alone in my room, but suddenly I felt so peaceful. It was an exquisite moment.

Have I struggled with sexual temptation and the urge to obsess sexually about people since then? Yes, of course. But that moment of surrender taught me that God doesn't run a mile from the stuff we find so hard to control. He's right there in the middle of it with us, offering us himself as the source of our deepest satisfaction.

Sexual purity isn't an easy idea to get our heads around in the day to day. Sexual purity isn't powerlessness. It's not anti-sex. It's not the absence of desire or the forerunner of shame. It allows us to freely celebrate the sheer wonder of female sexual desire as God created it. I think part of the problem we have with the whole P-word is that there are some terrible presentations of sexual purity out there: the married church leader continually shaming his wife for her sexual encounters before marriage as a way to help other women correct their promiscuous ways. More subtle, but no less damaging, is the young woman speaking of how 'above the whole sex thing' she is when in fact she's terrified she won't be able to get her sexual self back in the box if she admits her desires.

We are created to know deep desire. To be completely free in our expression of love and longing for the person we're in a covenant commitment with, the person we're married to. This is how God has made us to be – faithful and passionate in our desire for another, just as he is faithful and passionate in his desire for us. And knowing and embracing ourselves as sexual beings who ultimately long for God isn't put on hold until we find our partner. It's important for us to understand how God has made our bodies for love.

The big O

As women we have a number of erogenous zones where we can experience sexual pleasure: breasts, vagina, ears, neck and shoulders. But only one part of our body has no other practical purpose except pleasure, and that's the clitoris.

The clitoris has about 8,000 nerve endings, while the penis has only about 4,000. But unlike the penis, which hangs outside of the body, we can only see a small part of the clitoris as the rest is located inside our bodies. The 'rest' has great names like clitoral shaft, the urethral sponge, erectile tissue, glands, vestibular bulbs and the crura. And although small, the clitoris lets off powerful sensations that can spread across a woman's pelvic area by affecting 15,000 other nerve endings. Of course, we can't talk about the clitoris without talking about orgasm.

A recent study, reported in *New Scientist* magazine,[4] discovered that the female orgasm is truly mind-blowing. It activates the same part of the brain involved in out-of-body experiences. There comes a point in orgasm when you are taken out of yourself and where, for a moment, you feel no fear, only surrender. All this puts paid to the myths in culture that women's ability to feel sexual pleasure is somehow less than men's. Being able to feel sexual pleasure in our bodies is a beautiful gift of God that we can celebrate as a sacred, mysterious and wonderful part of being women.

There's a book in the Bible that still takes my breath away because it celebrates the mystery of sexual desire. It's called the Song of Solomon, but it opens with the song of a woman, intoxicated with desire for her lover. Here's how it begins:

'Let him kiss me with the kisses of his mouth!'
Song of Solomon 1:2, NIV

When we first hear her voice she's young and beginning to fall in love but unsure of what giving in to erotic pleasure might mean. She clings on to her lover when they're together and is in desperate agony when they're apart. It's a love that is fierce, but fragile. As the story develops we see a change in her as she begins fighting for him and for their love. She has long moments away from him that build resilience deep within her. Confident in their love, she's not afraid when they're apart, knowing that he will come back for her. And he does. But this time it's she who takes the lead. It's her voice we hear inviting them into the moment of complete surrender where they will become one flesh.

> 'Come, my beloved, let us go out into the fields and lodge in the villages; let us go out early to the vineyards, and see whether the vines have budded, whether the grape blossoms have opened and the pomegranates are in bloom. There I will give you my love.'
>
> Song of Solomon 7:11–12, ESV

This is a brilliant picture of sexuality, where two people mature in their love for each other so that they're neither enslaved nor inhibited by their desire. This is a love that has a future. It may be exclusive, but it's not secretive and shameful. It is a picture of sexual desire that is true, good and beautiful.

So often in the church we women are made to feel that our bodies are devices that enslave men to their dangerous sexual desires – and guess what, in society we often hear the same thing! I meet many women who, somewhere along the line, have picked up the idea that we shouldn't think about sex or talk about sexual desires until we're safely married. But that doesn't help us understand ourselves fully. In fact, it can make us feel afraid of the thoughts or feelings we have that might be to do with sex. So here are some ideas to help you think about your own desires, how God can help shape them and how you will express them.

1. Put your thirst first

How self-indulgent is your desire for God?

Beyond wanting to know about God or to have him do something massive in your life, do you want him for *his* sake? Do you just seek his hand, or do you hunger for his face? So often we want the excitement of a spiritual encounter because we want the thrill of connection, but do we desire *him*? Even if we're not given the answers we're hoping for? Do we allow our pursuit of him to build deep resilience within us?

This was exactly my journey of desiring God. I loved what I got from him and I was sent into a downward spiral if I felt he wasn't hearing me. What brought the beginnings of change was a combination of growing up and spending time with women whose unfulfilled desires brought them to the place of hunger simply for God.

I began to seek God like that. Not for what he could do for me, but for who he is.

Do you need to crave God? Has your deep desire for him been side-tracked by desires for people who, as great as they are, can't possibly fulfil you in the way that God can? David, the poster-boy for misdirecting his sexual desire, is confronted by one of God's prophets and challenged over his affair with Bathsheba. He writes these words, recorded in Psalm 51 (*The Message*), that are full of desire – not just for oneness with God, but also for God to forgive him and restore him as a man who can know God fully and be in control of his desires.

> 'God, make a fresh start in me,
> shape a Genesis week from the chaos of my life.
> Don't throw me out with the trash,
> or fail to breathe holiness in me . . .
> I learned God-worship
> when my pride was shattered.
> Heart-shattered lives ready for love
> don't for a moment escape God's notice.'

In a moment of ecstasy the apostle Paul speaks like a besotted lover: 'I no longer live, but Christ lives in me' (Galatians 2:20, NIV). It's not just doctrinal fact, it's utter ecstasy that comes from knowing the difference being one with Jesus makes in his life. Why not get down on your knees and cry out to God? Put into words your desire for him. Speak out the truth that you desire him the most. If you like music why not play something that draws your emotions in line with what your will is saying? When you're lost in worship, maybe with your arms wide open, and the music is pouring over you, what do you want in that moment? More than anything, I want to be one with God. I want to know no fear, no holding back. To know that I'm fully loved and accepted.

2. Don't rush

Sexual awakening is a process. It's about being woken up to a new state of awareness. The books I read certainly propelled my sexual awakening. Contrary to what popular culture might say, you don't need to rush into this. But I want to encourage you to have your eyes open to how your sexual self is developing, and how it is happening. Your sexuality is precious to God. Cherish your sexual self too.

Take a look at the sexual stimulation you're exposed to, whether it's what you're reading, looking at or doing. How is it affecting you? If you're already married, how are these ideas and images about sexual intimacy having an impact on your sexual disclosure with your partner? Where is it raising barriers between the two of you? What might you and your partner do to recapture sexual intimacy that is true, good and beautiful?

You may be a virgin. It's a difficult word to define in today's world of wall to wall digital sexual content. I define virginity as that state of never having had consensual sexual intercourse. I use the word 'consensual' because there are experiences of sexual intercourse that are against our will. I believe virginity in women and men to be an active choice that demonstrates a desire to not be united in one flesh with someone outside of covenant marriage. It's about honouring God, not just that you haven't had any sex yet! Being sexually innocent is a virtue, not an embarrassment.

If you are a virgin, how can you manage your own sexual awakening? I don't believe it's about keeping yourself in a state of sexual ignorance. Learn about your body, think about how your body responds to sexual stimulation in the media, arts or literature. Then set boundaries that demonstrate your respect for your sexual innocence. This empowers you to bring into your sexual self things that enable you to express your sexuality in ways that are true, good and beautiful.

You may have had sex or sexual experiences. So often we don't know what to do with these experiences – should we regret them, or learn from them? You might also be nursing some heartache or disappointment in the relationship or even in yourself. First, it matters that you're kind to yourself. Nothing can diminish the immense worth and value that God places on your life. When we shame ourselves for things we've done, we make it difficult to process what really happened. It might be that you had sex because you thought there was a commitment, or it might have been a casual thing. It's important to bring everything to God and ask him to show you where you need to know his forgiveness or reassurance that you are loved and precious to him. Secondly, draw a line under what's gone before – you don't need to keep reminding yourself of the mistakes you've made. Then thirdly, allow yourself time to think about what you want to do differently as you move forward. You are free to decide, not slide into situations. Who could you chat this through with? Allow the journey you've been on to empower your longing for God to direct your desires in ways that honour him and protect you from slipping into sexual relationships where there is no life-long commitment.

Maybe you're dating someone and you feel things are moving too quickly. There's something so intoxicating about the first few weeks of a new relationship! But it's important that at some point things settle down so that you can both take a deep breath and take in the mystery of the person you're in a relationship with. Dating doesn't exist in the Bible as it's a modern phenomenon, but I have no doubt that God is very positive about dating as a context in which you can explore what it takes to build a relationship that could one day become one flesh. Dating isn't marriage, but the vision of marriage is what you're measuring your relationship potential against. So how are the ways you're expressing desire to each other making it easier or more difficult to demonstrate true, good and beautiful self-giving love, both to them *and* to the person you may go on to marry in the future?

3. Love, don't lust

Each one of us has an internal battle between love and lust. Sometimes it can be so difficult to spot the difference between the feelings of lust and love. Lust impels us towards sexual intimacy with someone for what we think we will get from it. But lust isn't love, and we are created for self-giving love. Lust doesn't lead us to love. If sexual intimacy comes from nothing more than lust, it's not love. Love is different. Love impels us towards intimacy with someone for what we can give to them. It still feels like an over-whelming desire, but it's not one we're controlled by. The desire that has been checked by the Spirit of God helps us to see sexual intimacy as the place of self-giving love within marriage. It's an urge we are not controlled by.

Increasingly, after any talks on sex I give at Christian

events, young women wait to speak to me about mastur-bation. Sometimes porn is involved. Some of them struggle to say the word – they're so ashamed of what they've seen and the strong sexual desires they experience.

But I want to say that masturbation isn't a big deal.

In the grand scheme of things, touching yourself and bringing yourself to an orgasm isn't the end of the world. Exploring your own erogenous zones isn't an act of rebel-lion against God. So many Christian women feel passive in their married sex lives because they don't feel in control of their bodies. But ultimately sex with yourself is limited because it's not the context in which God intends us to experience the self-giving love that desire impels us towards. Because of that, it's not a pattern of behaviour you want to establish for yourself. It won't fulfil your sexual desires.

One option is to say, 'What the heck? Just get over it and on with it and don't worry so much.'

But that doesn't work because our sexuality is rooted in our deep humanity, so we bring the whole of ourselves to the sexual acts we do, whether we're aware of that or not. Masturbation ultimately feels like an isolated, lonely thing to do, because it *is*. So is having sex in each new relationship before we've decided if we're safe and free to disclose our very selves to this person – and them to us.

Some couples choose not to have penetrative sex before marriage but may mutually masturbate. It might be two bodies rather than one body and a sex toy, but it's still not self-giving love. It's a fake kind of closeness. For married couples who struggle with sexual penetration (for a whole host of reasons), sexual contact with each other is a precious and important way to remain deeply intimate in their one flesh. But I'd advise couples who are not in a covenant relationship to pay attention to whether they're setting up complicated rules that essentially are just about making sure they can still get off without getting caught out!

4. Desire or arousal?

Desire is wanting to have sex, and arousal is the ability for your body to respond and get turned on. Understanding the difference really helps, both if you're wanting to put boundaries around how sexually intimate you are with your partner before marriage and if you're wanting to deepen your sex life with your spouse.

Wanting to have great sex is a good desire to have. This desire needs to be in check because there might be people you want to have sex with but having sex with them wouldn't be safe, wise or legal. Arousal is the body's response to the desire to want to have sex and different things arouse different people. Although not really the kind of topic for everyday conversation, it does matter that as women we understand what taps into our own potential to experience and express erotic love. For one woman, physical comfort and protection from a partner arouses her body to be ready to experience deep sexual pleasure. For another woman, doing something physically demanding like rock climbing or running might have her ready for sex. For yet another it's seeing someone leading worship or cuddling a baby!

It's good to know how you become aroused so that you can either do it more with someone you can express erotic love with, or limit it. Instead of being repressive, this kind of self-awareness with the eyes of love can be incredibly empowering and freeing.

5. Plan for purity

Don't be afraid of the truth – it's what sets us free. God's truth is that where we feel most weak or unable to help ourselves, he is completely able to prove his formidable strength. Paul heard God say this to him, when he regularly faced something that threatened to hold him back from his desire to serve Jesus.

'I begged the Lord three times to take this problem away from me. But he said to me, "My grace is enough for you. When you are weak, my power is made perfect in you"' (2 Corinthians 12:8–9, NCV).

One thing God does is strengthen us to know in our hearts, define in our minds and act with our bodies the things we will or will not do. These are our God-given practices of abstinence and engagement. Below is an activity you might find helpful as you pursue a life of healthy desire.

Draw a vanishing point on a piece of paper (two lines joining at a point in the distance). At the vanishing point write in one sentence something you appreciate about being a sexual person. For example:

I can know and be fully known.
I am desired by God.
God made me sexual.
I can honour God with my sexuality.

Then on one of the lines to the vanishing point write the sentence 'My practices of abstinence' and on the other write 'My practices of engagement'.

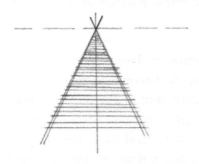

The deep belief that restraint isn't repression but the path to freedom is a powerful part of our understanding of what it means to be human. So it needs to be part of how we live our lives. Choosing the discipline of abstinence (where will I set my limits?) creates space to develop the skills of engagement (what practices and habits will I say yes to?).

MY PRACTICES OF ABSTINENCE
Write down some patterns of behaviour and habits that you will choose to avoid to pursue a sexually pure life.
    I will say no or not yet to the following . . .

MY PRACTICES OF ENGAGEMENT
Write down some patterns of behaviour and habits that you will say yes to.
    I will say yes to the following . . .

These lists of practices will be unique to you, and I recommend you share both with someone who respects you and has some theological understanding. Ask them to help you determine whether your lists are realistic, beneficial and positive about yourself as a sexual woman loved by God.

In 525 in Ireland, a slave woman gave birth to a little girl who grew up to become St Brigid of Gael, the patron saint of Ireland (and of the women whom their community called 'fallen' because of their own choices or men's abuse of them). Legend has it that when she took the veil to become a nun a flame of fire rose from her head. By mistake (or prompted by God?) the presiding bishop spoke over her the words to ordain her to become a *bishop*, not a nun. So as you seek to let God inspire and check your desires, receive these ancient words from one fierce female heart to another.

> 'I arise today
> Through a mighty strength:
> God's power to guide me,
> God's might to uphold me,
> God's eyes to watch over me;
> God's ear to hear me,
> God's word to give me speech,
> God's hand to guard me,
> God's way to lie before me,
> God's shield to shelter me,
> God's host to secure me.'

Brigid of Gael[5]

De-construct me

We have egos that don't want us to make changes to the habits or ways we've handled our desires up until now. Our ego, sometimes referred to as our 'false self', wants to guarantee our self-importance and protect our interests. And our ego is often in direct conflict with what we know we need to do.

But our egos aren't in charge – Jesus is! And he wants life to flow through you as you allow his Spirit to check your desires. So be honest about the things on your 'Practices of Abstinence' list that you're feeling resistance over. Ask God to help you identify why there is a battle in you over them. God has already won the victory over everything that would seek to take you down or keep you in shame, which means you don't need to fight. You need to invite the Spirit to increase your desire for God and set up some accountability in your life to help you develop new habits.

Re-construct me

You are created to feel deep desire, both for God and for other people. Being a woman who is embracing purity as a way of life doesn't mean that you ignore or repress your desires. Instead it means that you're willing to direct your desires for intimacy and connection in ways that allow you to live an expansive life in a way that honours God. Whether you're in a romantic relationship or not it's good to make sure you're regularly connecting with what your desires are telling you about what you need, both from God as well as from the people you are committed to.

To help you do this, why not spend time defining some of your 'Practices of Engagement'?

First, what helps you to connect with your desire for God? List two things you could commit to doing over the next few weeks to help fuel your passion for deeper intimacy with God. Try and think outside of the box and for things that are unique to you. For example, it might be sleeping under the stars, starting each day listening to a certain piece of music, finding an empty car park or field and dancing with all your might! Fill them in below.

For the next season, these will be my practices to help me engage with my desire for God . . .

1. ....

2. ....

Second, what helps you to connect with your desires for intimacy with your friends? Again, list two things you could commit to doing over the next few weeks to deepen your relationships. For example, it might be having a meal together once a week where you all bring something to eat as well as something personal to share, or setting up a WhatsApp group with friends where you can share Bible verses, prayers and encouragement. Fill them in below.

For the next season, these will be my practices to help me engage with my desire for deeper friendships . . .

1. ....

2. ....

Third, think about what helps you to desire to be sexually pure in your intimate relationships. For example, it might be regularly meeting a friend who encourages you to keep going as well as asking the difficult questions of account-ability or revisiting the story of a woman who inspires you in the way she handles herself sexually. Fill them in below.

For the next season, these will be my practices to help me engage with my desire for sexual purity . . .

1. ....

2. ....

3.

CLOSE

I'm a city girl. But one of the downsides of city living is light pollution – which means I rarely get to see the stars. So sometimes I jump in the car and head out into the country, star hunting. I'm awe-struck by the fact that these tiny pinpricks of light are millions of years away. How can something so distant be so captivating?

God counts the stars. He is the God who is always close to his creation: sustaining it, holding it, woven through it. Gazing up into the night sky I have an overwhelming sense of being swept up into the expanse of God. You can't gaze up at the night sky and think of yourself as anything but small, and you can't gaze up at the night sky and think of God as anything but huge beyond imagining.

Sometimes we need to sit in the presence of things that are light years away.

> 'In one hand he holds deep caves and caverns,
> in the other hand grasps the high mountains.
> He made Ocean—he owns it!
> His hands sculpted Earth!
> So come, let us worship: bow before him,
> on your knees before GOD, who made us!'
>
> Psalm 95:5–7, *The Message*

And sometimes things that are distant can help us to understand what's close to us. It's impossible to live life just gazing at stars because ultimately you and I were created for closeness.

God is close. He may hold the whole universe in his hand, but he is with you right now, closer than your skin, even closer than your breath. God created you for himself because he wanted to be with you. This God who is outside of space and time loves to be close to you; for there to be no time and space between you and him. He wants you to live in the closeness of his presence all the time.

> 'And I'll be right there with her . . . a wall of fire around
> unwalled Jerusalem and a radiant presence within.'
>
> Zechariah 2:5, *The Message*

This takes my breath away. God longs to be a wall of fire around me and a radiant presence within me. How incredible that he wants to be close to us like that. But it's a closeness with a purpose, because there's a whole world out there that needs to know God's closeness. To do that, they need *you* to get close to them.

Closer?

How do you feel about getting close to people?

I guess there are some you'd feel happy about and others you'd rather steer clear of. There might be legitimate reasons for this. But what if there aren't? What if your fear of getting close to someone is less about being wise for your own safety, and more about not wanting to feel challenged or uncomfortable?

Whether it's 'unfriending' someone whose views we don't like or shunning someone who doesn't bring anything we consider to be of value to our lives, our behaviour reveals our true priorities. Don't get me wrong: not everyone needs unfettered access to our attention and energy, but it's amazing how easily we can justify walking or turning away from people who are a bit difficult to get on with or love.

Last night I spent the evening with a young woman I've mentored since she was thirteen. She was back from university and in response to my question about what I could pray for her, told me how much she was struggling to spend time with some of the people in the flat at her halls of residence. 'I know they're the sort of people who need friends,' she confessed, 'but I don't always want to reach out to them. I'd much rather be doing something else.' As we prayed, it became clear to her that God was keen for her to find more ways to express love to them. She's gone back to uni armed with ideas for community meals and a deep conviction that God has placed her in this particular flat to be his hands and feet.

But it's not just individuals who struggle to get close to people who feel so far from God. Whole churches can too.

There's a church building on a housing estate that I know of with high numbers of unemployed adults, displaced families, lonely elderly people, struggling lone parents, kids truanting from school and crime. But the only part of this sentence the church cared about was the last word – crime. They're so terrified of having stuff damaged or nicked that they wrapped their church in barbed wire – literally. Great rolls of it, on the roof and brick wall that separated the church car park from the community who couldn't afford to drive.

You can imagine how that went down in the community!

A while back they asked me to preach. I didn't want to. In my view they blatantly didn't have any love for the people around them, so what on earth would we have to talk about? Then I felt the nudge of the Spirit to get close to these fearful people and tell them stories about the community around them. Many of these people used to live on the estate, but as they became more upwardly mobile they moved out to the suburbs, so each Sunday they drove to their church in a community they had become disconnected from. I knew the local school well from my days as a school youth worker. I knew some of the challenges people were facing, so I got up in the pulpit and told stories of the children and young people who lived just over the wall.

I talked about the girl growing up in poverty, not knowing that she should wear clean underwear every day and experiencing relentless bullying because of it. I talked about the elderly lady who never saw anyone from week to week. Stories of teachers crying because they knew the kids in their class weren't going to get any hot dinners during the school holidays. Absent dads. Alcoholism. Families having to choose between heating and eating. I even told them I knew of a group of young people who would sneak into the back hall of the church to stay safe and warm.

The ice around this church's heart began to thaw. The barbed wire came down.

When we follow Christ we are filled with the presence of a God who wants to get close to people. This means we can't follow Jesus and live at a distance from the very people God wants to reach through us. I have no doubt that as this fearful church opened their doors to their community, they experienced the powerful presence of Jesus in ways they had never known before.

It's easy to point fingers, and hard to ask ourselves in what ways we put distance between us and the people or communities Jesus might be eager to reach through us.

The trouble is that we tend to do fake closeness really well. We don't mean to! It's often the little bits of proximity we experience that can blind us to the call of Jesus to choose closeness over comfort. There's nothing wrong and everything brilliant about a week's mission in a different country or the occasional bit of volunteering at our local food bank. But these aren't the extent of what we're called to. Allowing these experiences to fuel your passion is a great start to inspire you to get as close as you can for as long as you can to the point of need.

Making the move

I recently stumbled across a story of a mother and son that took my breath away.

'We can't fully understand anything of importance from a distance,' Alice told her fourteen-year-old son, Bryan

Stevenson, and he never forgot it. Years later, while working as a hugely successful lawyer in New York, he took these words to heart and moved to Montgomery, Alabama. Years of defending men on death row had placed within him a deep desire to change the systems of poverty and abuse that plagued the communities these men came from. But he couldn't do this from the privilege and affluence of uptown New York, so he moved – to be physically close to those who needed this change the most.

Taking his body to a whole new space provoked systemic change. Turning up and being seen in a place of powerlessness and pain began a movement for change that continues to save people's lives today. He has worked on cases that have saved dozens of prisoners from the death penalty, helped to achieve court decisions to prevent sentencing under eighteen-year-olds to death and developed community-based reform of the criminal justice system, all because, as he says,

'The ideas in our minds are not enough to change the world, because it's really what's in your heart that gets you to do the things that seem a little dangerous, that seem a little edgy, that push you into these spaces that are uncomfortable. Ideas are meaningless unless fueled by some conviction in our hearts.'[1]

He's right.

We tend to understand the heart as the seat of our emotions. We see love hearts everywhere and can 'like' (tap on a heart icon) anything on social media that takes our fancy. But the ancients understood the heart as the essential self – the core of who we are. So when our hearts are moved by the need we see around us, our bodies have to respond, because we are one integrated being. Conviction in our heart means the possibility that a new way of living has just opened up to us.

People who use their bodies to live out their God-convictions are inspiring. Jackie Pullinger lives among the illegal drug dependent in Hong Kong, Danielle Strickland lives alongside the forgotten sex workers in Canada and Mother Teresa bound her life to the poorest in Calcutta. They're all women who have chosen closeness to people who need Jesus most, over comfort. In a world where everything screams at us, 'You deserve the best!' these women are radicals, reminding us that true liberation doesn't come from building your personal brand, but by giving up your life in the service of others. If fear of losing our comfort or even our lives doesn't stop us from drawing close to the people who need God most, then who and what possibly can?

'Don't be bluffed into silence by the threats of bullies. There's nothing they can do to your soul, your core being. Save your fear for God, who holds your entire life – body and soul – in his hands.'

Matthew 10:28, *The Message*

I've discovered that more often than not, what holds us back from getting close to others is our own selves.

Have you ever heard yourself utter the words 'It's not fair!'? When I bemoan the lack of fairness in the world it's more often than not because I didn't get something I felt entitled to – a parking space at the shopping centre on Christmas Eve; a same-day appointment to see the doctor; or enough money to buy a fifth pair of shoes. You know the score. Basically the kinds of privileges that I take for granted and that would be way beyond the reach of women in the two-thirds world. Behaving like this reveals how hard I've fallen for the idea that I'm entitled to status and comfort.

You may not consider yourself to be living a life of luxury, but so much of the time we are encouraged to be blissfully unaware of the comfort that cocoons our lives. In the West we have free access to things we consider ourselves entitled to: clean water, electricity, broadband, healthcare, education, protection under the law. All of this is ours, and not through anything we've done, but simply because we were born in the twenty-first century in a Western nation. This fact alone makes us women of privilege – whether we like that label or not. And with privilege always comes responsibility.

Hold yourself in that thought for a moment.

And most of us carry around further privilege of some kind. What's yours? Privilege simply means thinking about the ways we may, unwittingly, have an unearned advantage over other people. It might be down to our race, sexuality, background, education or postcode. It isn't because we necessarily value these aspects of our identity more than other people's identity, but because we live in a society that does.

For instance, I'm a straight, white, able-bodied and educated woman. These are facts that I can't change and although I've had to deal with sexism (mainly in the church) I've never encountered discrimination on the grounds of my skin colour or sexuality. My privilege isn't anything to apologise for, but it is my God-given responsibility to investigate and do something about it.

I'm *not* going to assume that you've got an easy life. You might even be experiencing some of the discrimination I'm writing about. But if like me you're living in the West, you have it so much better than most of the world's population. It's vital that in following Jesus we dare to ask ourselves how we can turn our unearned advantage into a source of blessing for others. An often-ignored part of the good news is that our dreams for an easy life were jettisoned the moment we decided to follow Jesus. The other bit of good news is that he's pretty brilliant at drawing people out of comfort and into good risk as he calls us to the adventure of opening our eyes to injustice and our hearts to those who need us to get close.

Visibility

I don't doubt that you are someone others look *at* and look *to*. Do you own a phone? Do you have any followers on social media? Are you part of a team at church? Do you have a bank account in your own name? If you called your church or small group leader about something, would they listen to what you had to say? Do you have leadership responsibility at work, college or university? No matter how limited you feel you are, you can you use your body – your visibility and voice – to help people in power to see those who are invisible.

Sometimes it requires us to take that first step of

choosing to open our eyes to other people's lives to see how much power we do have. I spent a few days in Moldova visiting a youth charity that supports young women who have been sexually abused and trafficked by gangs of men. I heard stories of mothers 'selling' their daughters for money to feed and house the rest of the family; young women, seriously addicted to using drugs and alcohol to numb the shame and torment of the abuse they were subjected to; parents, leaving their kids with grandparents for months or years on end, to travel to other countries for work. I sat with women of my age and younger who support these communities, and couldn't believe what I was hearing. I went to bed overwhelmed by the need and devastated by how powerless I felt to do anything.

That night I was woken up by an earthquake. It was terrifying. But what affected me most was that I felt a fraud asking God to keep me safe when I was in a country where all around me women and girls on a daily basis were trapped in systems of violence and abuse. Who was listening to their cries? How could God be listening to my pathetic cries for help when I was doing nothing on behalf of these women?

God did hear my cries and he did comfort me in my distress that night. He's a good Father who doesn't weigh up our needs against people worse off than us and decide who to love most – thank God! But I came home with a fire in my belly to *see* the privilege I have and use my body to shed a light on those that no one is looking at. If you and I have the opportunity to use our bodies for the sake of vulnerable people, I believe we're compelled to do it.

You're in control of where your body goes and what it

can make possible for other people. Of course, we're all limited by finances and opportunities, but probably not so much as we imagine. Think about all the smaller but significant choices you make about where your body goes: do you take a bus or hitch a lift? Do you sleep in his bed or on the sofa? Do you stop and help or look the other way?

These seemingly small choices add up to habits and disciplines that speak volumes about who we are and who we worship. Using our bodies powerfully as vehicles of hope, purity and justice bears witness to the God who came close to us in Jesus.

So who inspires you in the way they use their bodies?

One of my heroines is Gladys Aylward. Born in 1902 into a working-class family, no one imagined that this little girl had it in her to become one of the most influential missionaries the world has ever known. Aged eighteen she gave her life to Christ and felt a strong calling to become a missionary in China. But frustratingly she was turned down as a missionary, and as a single woman the prospect of moving to war-torn China felt like an impossibility. I'm so inspired by her tenacity. She didn't let anyone else's ideas on who and what she should be stop her. One day while reading the first chapter of Nehemiah she heard God speak to her, asking her if Nehemiah's God was her God. 'Yes, of course!' she replied. Then God told her to go to China.

'That settled everything for me. I believed these were my marching orders. I put my Bible on the bed, beside it my copy of *Daily Light*, and, at the side of that, all the money I had . . . and I said simply, "Oh God, here's the Bible about which I long to tell others, here's my *Daily Light* that every day will give me a new promise, and here is my money. If you want me, I am to China with these.'"[2]

God took her at her word. She spent the next year working tirelessly to get enough money to pay for her train ticket to China. She did it, and so began the long and difficult journey, alone. As a child I read a book about Gladys walking more than a hundred displaced children across the mountains, without food and shelter, to escape to safety. The courage and tenacity of this woman took my breath away! The toll this took on her body meant that for the rest of her life she struggled with the consequences of pneumonia, but I have no doubt that she bore those scars on her body with so much joy. They were evidence that she was living the dream God gave her!

The presence in our lives of women who live well and boldly with their bodies is a gift from God.

Imagine standing in the middle of a room. You're alone, but you're not afraid. You're just experiencing what it feels like to be in your body. What can you feel on your skin? What can you feel in your bones? As you take in the whole of your body, from the top of your head to the tips of your toes, what do you become aware of?

You're about to invite some women to join you in the room. They're women who bring strength to your life. They might be living, or dead. This is *your* imagination, not a real situation, so go for it! Who do you want in the room with you? Name them. In my room I've got my mum, my granny, Gladys Aylward, Brené Brown and Maya Angelou. Abigail, Mary and Deborah from the Bible and my closest female friends too. Who do *you* want? She might be an author, or an artist whose work has touched you. She might be a close family member or a friend. She might be a figure from Scripture or history. She might know your name or she might have no idea who you are. But name her.

Now, take a look at these women. What does it feel like to have them so close to you?

One by one, they come and lay a hand on your body. One of them touches your forehead, another holds your hand, someone else puts both her hands on the small of your back. The gentle deliberate weight of their hands makes you feel safe and strong.

As you walk out of the room, alone, you still feel the imprint of their hands on you. Their words, loving compassion and belief in you travel with you into every room you enter or every stage you step up on. These are the women I call my 'sisterhood'. I'm so grateful to God for the many women, living and dead, whose wisdom, beauty and courage give me confidence to be bold in loving my body and loving others with my body. Their roar helps me roar. Their joy gives me hope. Their courage helps me to be fearless.

Hesed

There's a wonderful story in Scripture of the love between women. Three women, a mother and her two daughters-in-law, become widows, almost overnight. Theirs is a story set in the rigid world of its time where women were identified with the person they belonged to. They're 'othered' by a community that makes them destitute because if they don't belong to men, they don't belong to anyone. Everyone's expectation is that the two daughters-in-law, Ruth and Orpah, will quietly return to their families and try to rebuild their lives by finding new husbands. But no hope like this exists for Naomi. Orpah returns to her family, but Ruth chooses to stay with Naomi, who plans to return to the place of her birth. I *deeply* admire the way Ruth uses her body to defend and protect her mother-in-law, both from the poverty of widowhood, and also from the society that would deny women can make their way in the world outside of existing social structures.

'But Ruth replied, "Don't urge me to leave you or to turn back from you. Where you go I will go, and where you stay I will stay. Your people will be my people and your God my God."'

Ruth 1:16, NIV

What a powerful pledge from a 'powerless' woman!

Both vulnerable and courageous, Ruth demonstrates a tenacious capacity to act on behalf of others and a willingness to risk vulnerability to keep the last remaining member of her new family safe.

Later in the story wealthy landowner Boaz, Ruth's future husband, uses the word *hesed* to describe how she has excelled at showing 'loyal love' or 'loving kindness'. This is more than just a feeling; it's something that you do for people you don't owe anything to. Some Bible scholars say there's no more accurate way to understand the nature of God than by understanding *hesed* – we don't deserve God's loyal love, and yet we receive it. God declares himself to be 'abounding in steadfast love [*hesed*]' (Exodus 34:6, ESV). The story of Scripture is laced with God's *hesed*. Look how he clothes Adam and Eve in animal skin to protect them in the harsh climate outside of Eden, even though they disobeyed him (Genesis 3:21). *Hesed* is a favourite word for the psalmists as they consider its impact on their lives: 'Surely goodness and lovingkindness [*hesed*] will follow me all the days of my life' (Psalm 23:6, NASB). The prophets tell the people that not only does God show us loyal love, but wants us to show that to each other too. 'This is what the LORD of Heaven's Armies says, "Judge fairly, and show mercy and kindness [*hesed*] to one another"' (Zechariah 7:9, NLT).

And Ruth, an unmarried, poor, immigrant woman, embodies all of this. She showed loyal, steadfast love when no one was asking or demanding it of her. It was completely freely given. Women like Ruth humble us. Women like Ruth can change us. Women who act in love, even when they have no societal power or privilege, show us that nothing, not even our circumstances or status, can prevent us from loving those who need love the most.

If this is what Ruth could do, with the little she had, how much more can we, with the privileges and opportunities we have?

The fact is that who you and I choose to get close to has a direct impact on who we're becoming. If we're spending much of our time with women who live only for themselves we're at risk of orienting our lives in that direction. Flowers grow towards the light. You and I grow towards the stories we choose to inspire our lives with.

And like Ruth, we can be a catalyst for change and hope as we offer steadfast love to others.

How amazing that we can do this with our bodies!

Lean in to women who give *you* strength with their loyalty and love.

Lean in to women who need the strength of *your* loyalty and love.

God's presence has an effect on how you use your body and where you go. If you know that he is a wall of fire around you and a radiant presence within you, that knowledge will spill out of you. Walk tall, woman. Stand firm, friend. Lift your face and raise your voice, mighty warrior. Give yourself away without fear of losing status or missing out.

He is close.

De-construct me

As social beings we pick up what we see people around us doing. This is how we learn most things. But it means that we need to pay attention to what we're picking up from the people we're spending our time with. If you're watching a lot of make-up tutorials on YouTube, you'll probably be great at doing your make-up and you might become more critical about your own or other people's appearance. Simply not wanting to be influenced by something unhealthy or ungodly is not enough of a protection against being shaped by it; we need to make intelligent choices about what has the potential to shape our lives.

Here are some challenges for you:

- Think about a typical day of the week for you and what you might be picking up from the behaviour and attitudes of people around you. Whose negativity has a habit of getting you down? Have you reacted to a situation or person in a way that wasn't really 'you' because everyone around you was acting in a certain way?
- Do you need to rethink how influential some people are in your life? It might be because you feel you are being shaped into their image and not into who God has made you to be. Or when you're with them you struggle to know your own heart and mind. You might even make decisions when you're with them that you later regret. Are you happy with the level of power they have? Is God happy with it? Ask God to help you know how to be wise in this friendship or relationship.

Re-construct me

Here are some more challenges:

- Look for a woman with more maturity and spiritual insight than you, whom you could 'lean into'. Ask if she would be willing to pray and chat with you as you seek to use your body for God's glory and to bring hope and strength to others.
- Look for a woman you could bless. You might feel able to offer to meet up once a month for a year, or you might like to make it a habit to prayerfully speak encouragement into the lives of women you know.
- Become more aware of women's lives in other commu-

nities and countries. When you hear the news of a disaster or a war somewhere in the world, find out and champion support for the women and children who are caught up in these situations.

• Make a point of getting to know what's happening for women in your university, workplace, college, community. Ask God to show you what you could do to use who you are and what you have to bless other women.

MIND.

'Lock up your libraries if you like; but there is no gate, no lock, no bolt that you can set upon the freedom of my mind.'

Virginia Woolf, *A Room of One's Own*

'But we have the mind of Christ.'

1 Corinthians 2:16, NIV

4.

FEAR

I was falling for Jason. There was a lot going for him. His northern charm and bad-boy past had me hooked. So when he suggested a drink down the pub I didn't hesitate, dragging my reluctant roommate Becca along with me for support.

On the way back to our halls of residence we took a short cut through a creepy graveyard. It was dark. Jason walked ahead of us, leading the way. Becca and I held on to each other in the darkness, tripping over headstones and giggling at how spooky it felt. Suddenly, a little ahead of us Jason stopped. We stopped too, and waited. Then after what felt like an age Jason spoke into the darkness, 'We have come. I have brought them.'

Silence.

Then nothing but our high-pitched screams and Jason's hoots of laughter at how successful his prank had turned out! Of course there was no one there. But for the briefest of moments I had felt the cold hard grip of fear around my neck. All the best scenes from the worst horror films crashed into my mind. Maybe this guy I was falling for was in fact in the service of a Dark Lord in some weirdo cult.

He wasn't. Sorry if that disappoints you!

Sometimes what we're most afraid of is the hidden

horrors around us. The uncertainty lurking in the shadows. The sickness, disappointment, failure, pain or bad news we sense to be hovering just out of sight. This is a terrorist's greatest weapon – randomly and senselessly attacking people as they go about their everyday lives is the surest way to instil fear into the hearts and imaginations of a whole population. It's little wonder that foreboding has become the feature of our age. We're more apprehensive, suspicious and uneasy as we go about our lives than our mothers' generation.

But it's not just the unknown that can make us feel afraid. Knowing that something bad is about to happen doesn't make us fear it any less. Certainty doesn't bring comfort. Have you ever stood waiting outside an exam hall or been ushered into the dentist's chair to get a tooth removed? Knowing what's about to happen doesn't make it any less terrifying! Friends of mine who have given birth more than once echo this. First time round they didn't really know what to expect (well, science lessons at school and the TV programme *One Born Every Minute* gave them some idea), but the second time was another story. One friend told me, 'Although I knew that once the baby was born all the contractions would stop, that didn't stop me worrying about going through it all again. I really wanted to un-know what I knew!'

But we can't. Sometimes we have to face our fear.

Sandpits and night terrors

Every summer my adopted daughter begs me to get the sandpit out. I dread this moment. Not because I have anything against sandpits, but because I have everything against the evil creatures that dwell under the decking and around the back of the shed where the sandpit is stored during the quiet cold months. Undisturbed all winter, the rats have been multiplying and gathering a whole host of nocturnal nasties that the rest of the year I like to pretend don't exist: big-eyed bugs, worms, the odd grass snake, a freakishly big spider. I know that tugging and dragging that sandpit into the light will wake these creatures up, and why on earth would I ever want to do that? But I grab my daughter, put on thick biker gloves, pick up a stick and head for the shed. Why? Because I'm a mum and it's what exasperated parents do to stop their kids whining!

And also . . . because I want to do some damage to the fear that would stop me doing the right thing.

I'm prone to caving in to fear. I can't tell you the number of times I haven't done something because I'm afraid of getting it wrong. But I don't want to belong to my fear; I want to belong to God. And the sandpit battle gives me a yearly reminder that if you're about to face your fears, don't do it alone.

That's the thing about fear. It can make us feel very alone.

Do you remember having nightmares as a child? More than anything you want someone you feel safe with to be there with you. Their presence matters. I don't know if you had a parent who was really good at chasing nightmares out of the window or 'sprayed' your room with nightmare-disappearing dust or maybe simply prayed with you (possibly the best option)! Having someone you love take control over something that feels out of control can be really comforting when you're six years old and frightened of snakes under the bed.

But as we get older we face the reality of nightmares that we can't chase out of the window or always wake up from. We might still be scared of snakes, but they're the least of our worries.

How do you get on with the news? I try and engage with world events every day. Sometimes the biased reporting or the stories that are omitted from the news feeds or headlines have me rolling my eyes. But mostly, tuning in to the stories of what is happening around the world has me on my knees, because our world is in pain. Seeing what's really going on around us can fill us with fear. Political unrest, nuclear threats, wars, global financial insecurity, environmental damage, people displacement, trauma and terror – where will this all lead? And what on earth can we do about it? Wherever you look there's so much to inspire our fear. I very much doubt I'm alone in feeling tempted to shove my fingers in my ears and sing 'La la la la la . . .' in the hope that all the bad stuff will just go away.

As I'm writing this a reworking of the reggae classic 'No woman, no cry' is being played on the radio. The haunting chorus, 'Every little thing is gonna be all right . . .', floats across the air. Does agreeing with this line put me into the camp of the blissfully ignorant, or the active optimists? I want everything to be all right, but I'm old enough to know that things don't always pan out as I hope. Bad things happen to good people. Things break, accidents happen, people get hurt.

So what do we do with that fact? What do we do with our fear?

For starters, Pinterest-optimism doesn't work. We don't fight fear with soundbites. Being told by celebrities surrounded by bodyguards, 'Don't let anyone make you afraid!' isn't helpful. Sometimes we just need to stop and acknowledge what we're afraid of.

New Testament theologian Tom Wright draws our attention to what he calls a 'surprising command': 'Do you know what the most frequent command in the Bible turns out to be? What instruction, what order, is given, again and again, by God, by angels, by Jesus, by prophets and apostles? . . . The most frequent command in the Bible is "Don't be afraid."'[1]

Is the fact that God knows we're fearful creatures who need to be told not to fear the surprising bit, or the number of times he's prepared to keep repeating it? Either way, God knows that we experience fear and anxiety, and he knows how much we need him to help us overcome our fear.

Short cuts and short-term solutions

During my life I've dabbled in a bit of Whac-a-mole praying! In case you didn't spend your teen years in the local gaming arcade, Whac-a-mole is a waist-high machine with a number of holes big enough for a puppet (normally one that looks vaguely like a mole) to randomly pop up through. You have a mallet and the task of hitting the 'mole' on the head every time it pops up. You're against the clock so the more times you hit the 'mole' the higher your score.

I didn't know I was doing it until I heard a brilliant sermon from American author and motivational speaker Priscilla Shirer at a leadership conference. She told the story of the time she queued with her son to play Whac-a-mole at the school summer fete. As Priscilla and her son watched the kids in the queue ahead of them play the game, her son grew increasingly frustrated. He couldn't understand why they kept knocking the puppets down only for them to pop back up through another hole. He felt so strongly about it that he marched to the front, pulled the sheet off the table and revealed the people under the table who were manipulating the puppets!

Priscilla was encouraging us to metaphorically pull back the sheet and wise up to the way the devil seeks to distract us from what God has already done in our lives. But I love this illustration as a way of thinking about how we're prone so often to dwelling in our fear. The enemy wants to keep you and me afraid. To make us believe our fears and to doubt that God is willing or able to protect and empower us through his Spirit at work in our lives. He wants you to doubt that you could be of any worth to God's kingdom, because that way you will just limp along in your timidity, afraid to become who you could be and to do the things you could accomplish in God's name.

We can spend all our time trying to prevent bad things from happening to us, or hiding away from anything that might make us feel afraid. We can wait until some situation or event grabs us around the heart to squeeze the hope and courage out of us before we ask God for his strength and his hope. But just like whacking the puppet

moles on their heads, these are all just short-term solutions and short cuts that don't get to the heart of the
matter. If we feel the prison of fear, we need to reach
for the one who gives us freedom through overcoming
our fears.

Anxious about anxiety

A while ago I got myself into a little bit of bother on
social media for suggesting that knowing Jesus means I
can be free from crippling fears and worries. Women
contacted me to question whether I thought that
Christians who felt anxiety or had some anxiety disorder
were somehow disobeying God. I quickly got back in
touch to say that in no way do I think that anxiety is a
sign of not loving Jesus enough. It is *never* my intention
to hurt people with my words. I learnt a lot that day
about the importance of recognising my privilege as an
able-bodied woman who doesn't suffer from a mental
illness. But I still stand by my conviction that God can
release us from everything that would hold us back from
living our lives.

So what do we do with anxiety? All of us feel anxious
from time to time, and everyday anxiety is a normal part
of life. It's the result of sensing that we may be at risk
of harm or pain. In fact, Jesus doesn't need to help us to
live anxiety-free, because anxiety is a gift from God. It
can play a protective role in our lives, warning us away
from harmful things. If you and I never felt any anxiety
we'd be a danger to ourselves and others. Being able
to assess the risk and potential for harm in any given

situation is an important part of life. If I had no sense that a heavy lorry could run me over, I might happily choose to eat my takeaway in the middle of the motorway. I would be risking my life for the simple fact that I wasn't able to focus on what was going on around me. Anxiety enables us to choose strategies to stay safe and minimise harm. But problems arise when our anxiety begins to spiral out of control, leading us to the kind of thinking that feels stuck and panic inducing. I believe that God can powerfully help us in these times because he can give us a deep sense of peace and security that enables us to face whatever is provoking our anxious thoughts. I can often feel overwhelming anxiety *after* I've preached or spoken at an event because I think that people are hating what I said or have been badly affected by something I didn't mean to say! I am learning to quickly recognise the signs that my anxiety is increasing (headache, restlessness, heart beating fast, negative thoughts going round and round in my head) and then I ask God to fill my mind and body with his peace and calm. In these moments (which can last a few hours) I reach into my mind for verses of Scripture that help me to focus on God's power and love, like: 'Give all your worries to him, because he cares about you' (1 Peter 5:7, NCV).

This is where fear and anxiety can feel very similar. But whereas anxiety is about a perceived threat or harm or pain, fear happens as a result of a real threat of pain or harm to us. There might be situations in your life that make you feel afraid. The reality that you might be ill, fail your exams, or lose your job, relationship or home can fill you with fear that can feel crippling and isolating.

But even as we face our fears, we are not alone. God finds us in our fear, and knows us in our fear.

The incarnation of Jesus speaks volumes about how God 'gets' fear. Nothing scares God. But Jesus, both fully human and fully divine, felt fear. Knowing that his torture and death were only hours away Jesus experienced acute fear and extreme distress. So much so that it brought on hematidrosis – a rare but serious medical condition, often observed in people awaiting execution, where sweat contains blood (Luke 22:44). Medical experts tell us what the Gospel authors wouldn't have known – that people who suffer from hematidrosis are also highly likely to experience intense headaches and abdominal pain. The result of the blood sweats is that skin feels fragile and tender for a while afterwards.

Simply writing these facts moves me to tears. We have a saviour, seated now in heaven and interceding before the Father on our behalf, who understands fear and pain on a personal and profound level. It wasn't just spiritual agony that Jesus felt on the cross. It was every physical pain and fear emotion we've ever felt. We can never say to Jesus, 'You don't know what this feels like!' He does. He went through with it anyway because he loves you and me.

That's how much God loves and knows you.

God finds you in your fear

One of my favourite stories about Jesus is also about fear.

He's just fed thousands of stranded people on a hillside with nothing more than one boy's packed lunch. Exhausted and in need of alone time with his Father,

Jesus sends his disciples off on a boat and heads up a mountain. A little while later, as he comes back down to the shoreline, he sees that the weather on the lake (think sea, not pond) has turned pretty nasty. Nonetheless he sets out to beat the disciples to the other side by walking on the water. Then there's an intriguing moment in the story where it's obvious that Jesus had no intention of being seen by the disciples. He makes as if to go past them, and only changes his course when he sees how terrified they are.

> 'Later that night, the boat was in the middle of the lake, and he was alone on land. He saw the disciples straining at the oars, because the wind was against them. Shortly before dawn he went out to them, walking on the lake. He was about to pass by them, but when they saw him walking on the lake, they thought he was a ghost. They cried out, because they all saw him and were terrified. Immediately he spoke to them and said, "Take courage! It is I. Don't be afraid." Then he climbed into the boat with them, and the wind died down.'
>
> Mark 6:47–51, NIV

Their fear is real. It's not a fear this time about the storm around them (although that may have heightened their stress and anxiety somewhat). We're told that they were afraid because they saw a ghostlike figure standing on the waves. God can be terrifying to behold sometimes. But instead of chastising them for their fears and asking them why they still don't get who he is and what he can do, Jesus defies the laws of nature and reaches them across the water, getting into their boat and bringing them safely to the shore. The source of their fear is also the source of their comfort.

What storms are raging in your life? In what ways is God doing things in your life that feel both comforting and terrifying at the same time? Where does fear loom large for you? Jesus has just joined you in the boat. How is that going to change things for you? Maybe he will stand up and speak to the waves: 'Peace, be still!' Maybe he will guide the boat to shore. Maybe he will get back out of the boat, and offer you his hand to join him on the waves. Who knows? He is God after all. He does what he does. But what he does is always to bring you into a closer intimacy with him.

God strengthens you to face your fears

A while ago I had a brush with cancer. My mum and grandmother both suffered with breast cancer, so when I felt the dull pain in my breasts and the tell-tale lumps, I hotfooted it down to the GP and was referred for tests. They found something suspicious. 'What's in there?' I asked my boobs one day as I stood naked in front of the bedroom mirror. 'I don't blame you girls. But if you know something I don't, now's the time to confess. I won't be cross.'

Silly me. Boobs can't talk.

A few days later I was in a day clinic to have some investigative surgery. Lying there, face down, waiting for the surgeon to get to work, I began to sift through my thoughts to find one I could grab on to. Like looking through a clothes rail at a vintage shop. This one? No, too many emotions linked to that. How about this? Gosh, no. Now the tears are rising, got to move on from that one. While I was shuffling through my thought rail, a nurse placed a box of tissues next to my face. It was beginning to hurt now. Quick! I needed to grab something to focus on. Then I saw it. The box of tissues. Why were they there? I wasn't crying. What did she know that I didn't? She knew that women who lay on this trolley, facing the fear of cancer, cry.

I can't tell you how much the thought that I was lying somewhere that women had cried moved me. I imagined reaching out to them to comfort them, so that they wouldn't be alone. That's when I felt the overwhelming comfort of God reaching out to me. Holding me steady. Helping me to look my fear in the face and know that whatever the damage or pain that might come God would never leave me. In that moment, his comfort felt more real to me than my fear.

I'm not much of a map reader. I prefer my trusted satnav that I've programmed with a gentle New Zealand lilt! But if you were living in medieval times and wanted a jaunt across the country you would discover something fascinating about how your peers viewed the surrounding landscape. Created with painstaking attention to detail and immense skill, medieval maps tell us about our ancestors' fears of the unknown as well as their knowledge of their physical environment. On a handful of maps that still exist, uncharted territories where no one had yet been are marked with the words 'Here Be Dragons'. More commonly, illustrations of monsters and wild beasts in those unknown places drive home the point that where there is uncertainty, there is terror.

As I lay on the trolley, in the hands of the surgeon, I discovered something wonderful. When you face the unknown in the hands of God, there are no dragons there. Whether there are boxes of tissues and kind women to hold your hand or not, there is always God. And where God is, there is freedom, peace and joy.

God walks with you to overcome fear

Have you ever done something really well? How did that feel? Great. If only we could succeed at everything all the time! It would be amazing to never have to deal with missing the mark or getting stuff wrong. The fear of failure motivates so many of our actions.

But ultimately we learn through failure. We *grow* through failure. There's no surer way to overcome fear than to absolutely totally and utterly fail, then realise God is still God and life carries on! There's nothing more humbling than knowing that you can do nothing without God's help. But leaning on God requires us to take risks. That's tough!

Years ago I founded a charity off the back of a TV documentary I was in. We took twelve North London teenagers through a nine-month sexual abstinence programme. It functioned a little bit like an AA group with the young participants signing a pledge and supporting each other in their experiment of delaying sex. As only one of these young people was a Christian, and he had come to faith through a sermon at his friend's church all about no sex outside of marriage, it made for fascinating discussions! It still remains one of the most incredible experiences of my life.

I had had no idea or intention of setting up a charity. But the impact on the twelve teenagers was so significant that it quickly became clear that we needed to find a way to empower other young people both outside and inside church to go on a similar journey. I quickly discovered that the nine months of filming and working with the young people was the easy bit. Running a charity was hard. As we'd started life with so much media coverage and platform at youth events, everyone thought we were rolling in funds. We weren't, and the endless rejections from trusts and wealthy individuals left me feeling a deep sense of failure. I had grown up in a family that never experienced financial security, and so each time I filled in a funding form or met a funder to ask for help, I felt like that homeless little girl again.

One day I was invited to a swanky hotel in London to meet a lovely guy who had been so encouraging to me in the first few years of running the Romance Academy. But understandably, his frustration at my lack of finding a way to increase cash flow into the charity had reached its limit. I remember him telling me straight up that I should just close the charity down. It wasn't going to work. A few weeks earlier my husband and I had been given the news that short of a miracle, I wasn't going to be able to conceive a baby.

Sitting in the hotel's wine bar on that grey afternoon, I felt as if all my failures were crashing down on me at once. I think I mumbled my thanks for his honesty and made my way down a spiral staircase to the loos. By the time I made it to a cubicle I was having a full blown panic attack. I couldn't stop shaking. The sobs were coming from my gut in loud rasps. My heart felt as if it would burst out of my chest and I thought there was something around my neck, restricting my breathing.

Incredibly, a wonderful member of the cleaning staff who couldn't speak much English saw me head down the stairs to the ladies' toilets in distress. She swooped in, found me on the floor and came back with the hotel manager. He took one look at me and brilliantly announced, 'Madam, you are suffering from shock and grief!' I still think it was the Spirit who spoke to me in that moment.

I remember thinking, *I am! I am! I'm a failure! I've always known it. I've always feared that others would discover it. And now it's out there. I'm a failure. God, don't use me. Don't ask for me. Please leave me alone.*

But God in his kindness didn't leave me alone. He provided this wonderful woman who couldn't speak to me, but who sat on the floor rubbing my back as the manager stuck a 'DO NOT ENTER' sign on the loo door and fled upstairs to call a paramedic. I often wonder if these kind people were in fact angels. But I guess that God sometimes chooses to use complete strangers to minister to us at the point of our greatest need.

I still weep my way through my failures. I still fear that my mess and mistakes might swallow me whole. Then I remember being on the floor in that posh London loo and vowing to let go and let God take my fears and fail-ures and use them for his purposes. If he could be strong when I was weak, I didn't need to be afraid of my weakness. I just had to keep saying, 'Yes, I'm afraid, but as God is with me, let's do this!'

The truth is that fear cannot co-exist with love. It's one or the other. A horrendous stench and an exquisite smell can't linger in the exact same space. Two conflicting ideas can't both be true; the world is either flat or it's spherical. It can't be flat *and* spherical. We either belong to our fear, or we belong to the God who loves us.

When it comes to fear and love, we can choose which one will take up more and more room in our minds. We do this by feeding the one we want to grow. This is not just down to our own mental capacity to think more about love than about fear; it happens as we allow God into our fears with his hope and love. As God takes up room in our lives, fear has less space to breathe. That's why Scripture tells us in no uncertain terms:

'God is love. When we take up permanent residence in a life of love, we live in God and God lives in us. This way, love has the run of the house, becomes at home and mature in us, so that we're free of worry on Judgment Day—our standing in the world is identical with Christ's. There is no room in love for fear. Well-formed love banishes fear. Since fear is crippling, a fearful life—fear of death, fear of judgment—is one not yet fully formed in love.'

1 John 4:17–18, *The Message*

John here is speaking about the two things we all crave: confidence to stand before God in our failure without receiving the judgement we deserve, and the secret to banishing fear from our lives. That's because they go together. Ultimately, all fear is the fear of judgement and death. Of being found out, rejected, abandoned, lost forever. John is saying that as Jesus has taken the weight of the judgement that should have been coming our way, we don't need to live under fear of what might happen to us any more. Even if we lose our lives, we are still held by God and have complete certainty that we will live with God for all eternity.

A few years ago our family took a trip to the north coast of Ireland. One afternoon while Jason was napping (he had already turned forty by this point and was milking it) I dragged our three-year-old out for a bracing stroll. All was well until we turned the corner. Houses gave way to an open horizon and we were met by the full impact of gale force winds pummelling the Causeway coastline.

I shoved my daughter behind me to stop her blowing away, and glared defiantly into the oncoming storm. It reminded me of that infamous 'You shall not pass' scene in *The Lord of the Rings* where Gandalf places himself between the Balrog and Frodo. It speaks to so many of us about those times we seek to stand in the gap for young people who are drowning in the storms of pain, rejection, addiction, abuse, despair. We recall stories of Jesus conquering the waves because they speak to us of the God who has defeated the one who would destroy humanity.

So I shouted to the sea, 'I'm not afraid of you. I'm loved by God and he stands in front of me. He takes the force of the blow. He shelters me. He fights for me. I don't need to be afraid!'

(I know. Crazy. But so liberating. You should try it!)

But for the rest of the day I was still restless. My pep talk hadn't quite got rid of all of my anxiety.

So later that evening I ventured out alone in the dark to the same spot. For a few breathless moments I flung my arms wide and gave in to the storm raging around me. I felt a kind of terror and peace. I suppose it was a moment of self-loss. Knowing that I could be swept away. Knowing that nothing exists in me that can be hidden from a holy God, but knowing also that instead of being dragged down into death, I am being swept up in the waves of God's infinite love.

In times of stress and anxiety, when things don't work out as we'd hoped, when we rock up and open up and still feel we've lost, we can take hold of God and all his promises that he will never abandon us. His perfect and infinite love for us drives out fear and makes it possible for us to grow in the confidence of who we are and how we are loved. I'm determined more than ever to recognise the ups and downs of the journey I've been on and the insecurities I still have, so that I never forget to make Jesus my centre. I'm practising the art of plugging in to the God who knows, loves and transforms me.

'She who dwells in the shelter of the Most High will rest in the shadow of the Almighty. I will say of the LORD, "He is my refuge and my fortress, my God, in whom I trust." . . . He will cover you with his feathers, and under his wings you will find refuge; his faithfulness will be your shield and rampart. You will not fear the terror of night, nor the arrow that flies by day, nor the pestilence that stalks in the darkness, nor the plague that destroys at midday. A thousand may fall at your side, ten thousand at your right hand, but it will not come near you . . . For he will command his angels concerning you, to guard you in all your ways . . . "Because she loves me," says the LORD, "I will rescue her; I will protect her, for she acknowledges my name. She will call upon me, and I will answer her; I will be with her in trouble, I will deliver her and honour her . . ."'

Adapted from Psalm 91:1–16, NIV

Of course it's easy to say and oh so tough to do. But as with all seemingly impossible things, all we need to do is take the next step. That often begins with asking Jesus to help us face the next ten seconds, then the next, then the next . . .

You can do it . . .

. . . because you're loved.

. . . because there are no dragons, only new things to discover.

. . . because where you lead, others will follow.

. . . because you don't belong to fear, you belong to God.

De-construct me

It can really help to name your worries and then explore what lies behind them. Sometimes I give myself space to 'catastrophise' my thoughts, which means that I think of something I'm anxious about and then ask, 'What's the worst that might happen?' I often find that taking my anxious thoughts captive in this way and talking my way to the conclusion of my worry can help me get some perspective on it. You could try it too.

Have there been times when what you've most been afraid of is God himself? Like the disciples seeing Jesus on the waves, we don't always know what God is up to, and that can make us feel anxious or afraid. Bring these anxieties to God too.

Re-construct me

God is the solid foundation for your life, and his love drives out your fear of being lost, invisible, easily replaceable or knowing only failure and despair. God's love is very real and we experience it in a whole range of ways that are unique to us. Dr Gary Chapman calls them our 'love languages'.[2] Take a look at the definitions of these love languages and think about which ones resonate with the way you give and receive love.

1. Words of affirmation – using words to affirm and validate someone.

2. Positive touch – this is consensual and loving, non-sexual touch, which communicates reassurance.

3. Quality time – giving the other person your undivided attention to show that right now they are the focus of your interest and affection.

4. Gifts – giving a thoughtful gift demonstrates that you have taken the time to think about someone and what they might like.

5. Acts of service – this is about showing with your actions that you value the other person.

You will find yourself leaning towards one or two of these ways of receiving (and giving) love more than the others. So think about the way you experience God's love for you – how might God be showing you his love through your love language? It might not be immediately obvious, so take some time to stop and ask yourself, 'How has God shown his love to me through words of affirmation [or whichever it is]?'

Once you know how you're mostly likely to experience love, pay attention to it and ask God to show you his love in this way.

Words of affirmation – who has God used recently to speak lovingly into your life? Or how has he spoken to you through what you've been reading in the Bible?

Positive touch – who has God used to reach out a hand to care for you, or to make you feel valued by their presence at a time when you needed to know you were not alone?

Quality time – when has God used a period of time in your life (a long coach journey or a walk by yourself) to give you a special sense of his presence, even if you can't put it into words?

Gifts – has God reminded you in some way recently of the grace he has poured into your life? Or has someone given you something that has helped you to connect with the knowledge that God cares for your needs?

Acts of service – maybe a stranger opened a door for you or someone you knew did a thoughtful thing for you without you asking, and God used it to remind you that he has surrounded your life with everyday blessings that you often overlook?

As you pay attention to the unique ways that God shows his love to you, invite his love to take up more room in your life.

5.

PERFECTION

'There is no perfection, only beautiful versions of broken-ness.'

Shannon L. Alder

Ophelia Vanity from California wants to be Barbie, which isn't low-cost or low-maintenance. Aged thirty Ophelia might be able to pull off the iconic doll look, but how about when she's fifty and her body struggles to support the punishing regime of bleaching, botox, dieting and procedures to be Barbie? It also begs the question of why anyone would go through all of this in the first place!

Because Barbie is 'perfect' and perfection comes with the promise of personal happiness. Or does it?

I really *really* dislike Barbie.

I remember once sharing my loathing with a bunch of little girls at the kids' group at church I was helping out with. We'd just finished the obligatory colouring sheet and had a bit of time to kill. More comfortable with teens than children at nursery school, I decided to open up a conversation about body image and the impact of the commercialisation of female identity on the self-esteem and expectations of young women! I had six pairs of eyes gazing up at me, wide-eyed in wonder at my tirade of complaints that ranged from Barbie's messed-up proportions ('If she was a *real* woman with that breast-to-feet-size ratio she wouldn't be able to stand upright') to the nihilistic, self-absorbed lifestyle depicted on her TV shows. 'But it's her *shape* that I detest the most, girls. It's just not *real*.' At which point one little girl put her hand up and protested, 'But she's got elbows and knees.'

I remember a friend of mine being an au pair for a four-year-old called Ella. Bathing her one night, my friend thought she'd contribute towards this little girl's positive body image. 'You know, Ella, you are beautiful, exactly as you are. It's OK to be any shape. Any shape at all.'

Ella thought for a moment. 'Can I be a triangle?' she asked.

I'm still too often a sucker for perfection – the belief that if my life, skin, relationship, job, house and hair were better, I'd be happier. In these moments I have the habit of setting my sights on some unattainable ideal I've stumbled across in an advert. It seems that although nothing in me wants to *be* Barbie, I'm as prone to the lie of perfection as Ophelia Vanity is. Why? Because like every other human being on the planet, I want to be happy.

Happiness. What makes you *truly* happy?

Most of us have a happiness philosophy. For some it's about experiencing as much pleasure as is humanly possible. For others it might be less about experience and more about accumulating things like the latest gadgets or that better house, car, job, clothing or holiday. Then of course there is relationships. They play a huge part in personal happiness. Many of us would willingly give up a life of wealth for a loving and lasting relationship. Or maybe we have this notion that happiness is simply what will invade our lives when everything is in place and life is exactly as we planned or hoped it would be. However we approach it, the pursuit of happiness gets a lot of airtime in our culture.

But it's hard to get away from the reality that most of the time many of us feel that whatever happiness is, it's evading us right now. We struggle to define it and we struggle to find it. On a survey we might tick the 'I'm OK' box, but dig a little deeper and it's not long before we find the discontent lurking inside.

Yet endlessly resourceful, we find ways to make ourselves happy. This is where perfection comes in, because in these happiness-seeking moments what we tend to go looking for is what we feel is lacking – whether it's inferiority about our looks, status, achievements or faith – and we go hard after the best version of it.

The voice of perfection

Perfection has a voice and it's mean! It tells us we're not good enough, not clever, thin, sexy or popular enough. It's a noisy voice that looms large in our minds when we're feeling tired, sad, hungry or lonely. And it's a voice that probably sounds like the person or people who have been the most critical of us as children.

'Do better. Try harder. Why can't you be more like your sister/brother/fish? I expected more from you and you gave me nothing. You just don't have it.'

I know I'm not alone in my battle with my inner critical

voice. I wonder who we're all comparing ourselves to – other women who are also battling their flaws on their path to happiness? Why do we fear being less than perfect when we know that perfection *doesn't exist*?

It's because we live in a society that acts as if perfection is real.

Check out the poisonous advertisement hoardings, female celebrity selfies, the Christian self-help 'I-don't-struggle-with-anything-anymore' books and blogs. Knowing that perfection isn't real isn't comforting in a society that makes out that people who matter most give a pretty good impression of having the perfect life. In fact, the moment you put that image of yourself with triple chins out on social media or tell your friends you're not sure God is listening to your prayers right now, you can find yourself the object of people's shaming for just being who you are or saying how you're feeling.

Or maybe you've had one of those unforgettable experiences where no matter how much time has passed since you kissed that guy and he told everyone it was like kissing a sock, the mere memory of it is loaded with such difficult emotions that you want to crawl under the duvet and binge-watch *Gilmore Girls* (or is that just me?). But there doesn't need to be a specific event in your past for the niggling fear that you just don't measure up to be lodged firmly in your mind.

One of the reasons that we don't always spot the critical inner voice of perfectionism is because we mix it up with our desire for excellence. But they're not the same. *Excellence* is about doing your best. You might be proud of the end result, or not, but you can rest assured that you tried your hardest and gave it all you had. You can pick yourself up, dust yourself off and hold your head up high. *Perfectionism*, on the other hand, means the job is never done, the situation is never good enough. There's always something more to try as you chase a continually moving goal. It can keep you in a perpetual state of exhausted hypervigilance.

And this battle is being fought in your mind.

We buy into the lie in our mind before we ever work it out in our body. When the idea that we need to be perfect takes root in our minds, it's not too great a leap to act in ways that would otherwise seem ludicrous to us. Like spending thousands on facial restructuring or going to great lengths to hide away our failures and insecurities.

Is everything really everything?

Today, girls in the UK can expect to grow into women who will lead in industry, fashion, church, education, arts, technology, medicine, the forces, security and politics because they're capable and work hard to achieve it. There's never been a time in human history where we have been given as much control over our choices as we have now. But with these everything-*possibilities* comes the potential for everything-*paralysis*. If you can do anything and be anyone, how do you *know* what and who you need to be? Where do you look for cues to help you decide? And what happens if you become someone or do something that looks, well, *ordinary*?

If you're responsible for your own happiness, what happens if you're not happy? Who do you blame?

Well, others for a start. People we know and people we don't. Social media provides us with a convenient vehicle for launching our complaints against other people who get in the way of our opportunities. In *Virtually You: The Dangerous Powers of the E-Personality*,[1] Elias Aboujaoude talks about the way internet technology exaggerates our cause, encouraging us to be more impatient and vicious in our communication, both on-line and off-line. We're quick to blame others for our discomfort, whether they're responsible for it or not.

It works. For a time. Offloading the blame for our discomfort onto others distracts us from wondering whether the problem lies with us. Are we quick to point the finger at everyone else because we know we're partly responsible for where we are? There's something called 'victim mentality' that happens when we find ourselves stuck in blame mode. We interpret situations from the perspective of being someone who everyone else is out to 'get'. I hear it in young teenagers a lot. 'My teacher hates me. That's why I threw a chair at her.' Her teacher might struggle with her behaviour and this teenager might well be feeling victimised and shamed each time she's in school. But if she carries this attitude into adult life, she is at risk of growing into a woman who struggles to take responsibility for her life and so is not able to take the opportunities that would lead to achievements and success. This isn't a judgement of the teenage girl. I'm right there with her working this through because I believe in the best for her! But it's an observation of what happens if we grow up feeling everything is always someone else's fault.

But back to happiness.

You may, like me, have wondered whether your lack of feeling completely content and happy with your situation is actually because you're just not good enough to be happy. Written out in black and white like this makes it seem an absurd suggestion. But I know I've thought it.

But there's good news, even if it doesn't immediately sound like good news.

The good news is that God has never promised that we would always be happy. This side of eternity, we won't be perfect either. It's good news because if God alone knows what we need and how we're made and *he's* not obsessed with making us happy, then maybe there's something more going on than we realise! (This isn't the same as saying that God wants us to be miserable or unfulfilled, by the way. Nothing could be further from the truth.)

So first up, *perfection*.

There is no ceiling above what I can achieve as I direct my energies and talents in the direction of my skills and abilities. But this doesn't mean I live with the fantasy that I can do and be whatever I want to be (remember the triangle?). For all the hard-won opportunities we have (and please make use of them), we all have limitations. They're mostly relational limitations. I'm someone's daughter, someone's wife, someone's mum, someone's friend. These limit me because I can't suddenly live as if all these identities don't matter any more. Well, I could. But the consequences would be devastating. There are also practical limitations. I might suddenly decide I want to be an astronaut. Great idea! But the reality is I don't have the time, intellect or willpower to really make that happen. Rather than spend the rest of my life despairing that I never got to walk on the moon, I can choose to pour myself into something that fits me. This isn't an argument against reaching for the stars, but it's a caution against sacrificing thriving at what I can do on the altar of perfection.

I don't need to walk on the moon to reach the stars!

You don't need to set your expectations to my limitations. If you reach for the stars and walk on the moon I will be cheering you on! But simply not reaching an arbitrary set of goals doesn't add up to an unfulfilled, meaningless life. Not when you know the God who gives all of life its meaning.

Secondly then, *happiness*.

You and I are not ultimately in control of our personal fulfilment. We can't be, because we're not God. We're the created, not the Creator. It means we don't need to have complete control over our lives. We don't need to fear that we're alone in our search for meaning and fulfilment. Our salvation is in his hands, in his blood. I'm not just talking about the gift of life after we die. I'm talking about being saved from the curse of being the authors and perfectors of our lives. That job has been given to someone else.

In his brilliant book *Making Sense of God* Timothy Keller defines the dead-end nature of being caught in striving for perfection like this:

'We want something that nothing in this life can give us. If we keep pursuing it in this world, it can make us driven, resentful, or self-hating. If we try to harden our hearts so that it doesn't bother us, we harm our humanity and those around us. If, however, we don't harden ourselves, and fully feel the grief of desire's lost hope, we may find self-destructive ways of drowning in it.'[2]

So what do we do?

Echo chamber

There's a children's story about a greedy rat that mindlessly steals from all the other animals. Sat astride his long-suffering horse, the Highway Rat demands pastries, cakes and buns from anyone he meets on the road. But no matter how many sweet treats he prises out of the hands of the beleaguered animals, he's never satisfied. Convinced that somewhere there is an endless supply of goodies, he's duped by the wily Duck into believing that the cave on the hill has what his heart desires. As he shouts his demands into the cave, he hears a voice call back to him. Convinced it's an invitation to eat until he can eat no more, he disappears into the darkness.

But of course, the voice he hears is just an echo of his own questions.

Which caves do you shout your longings for happiness and fulfilment into? Mine look like online shopping, a new project I can lose myself in or a package holiday that dazzles me with clever advertising. All these things are great gifts from God, but they're not God. What they provide will always be limited. Expecting a created thing to give me what only the Creator can is the root of idolatry.

'I want to be happy!' we cry.

'. . . be happy . . . be happy . . .' comes back the taunting echo.

'I want to be free!'
  '. . . be free . . . be free . . .'

'I don't think I can be perfect!'
  '. . . be perfect . . . be perfect . . .'

How do we silence our echo chamber? How do we enjoy the good gifts in life without putting them in the place of God?

A good start is listening to other people's voices: women and men, not just in our culture, but from all around the world, who have learned to surrender the false reality of perfection for a full life in Christ. Like Nazi concentration camp survivor Corrie Ten Boom who, now in heaven, speaks as someone who has experienced hell. Her secret to the good life? Making Jesus your prize.

> 'If you look at the world, you'll be distressed. If you look within, you'll be depressed. But if you look at Christ, you'll be at rest.'

We don't resist merely by changing our thinking, or through great acts of will. We've got to look deeper and ask God to help us direct our love to him. Here are some things I have found really helpful in my journey of loving my beautiful imperfections and asking Jesus to restore his image in me. The first three are outside-in operations and the last cuts right to the heart of the matter.

1. Spot the lie

First we need to recognise the pursuit of human perfection for what it is – a lie.

It's a lie because it is the false reality of a godless pursuit. The pursuit of it makes us dissatisfied with the things God has already given us or is doing in us. By chasing after what we think will make us happy, we're essentially saying to God that he is not enough for us and his plans are not the best for us.

The pursuit of human perfection also breeds in us an expectation of perfection from people around us. No one is perfect, except Christ. Expecting other people to take personal responsibility for themselves is realistic and kind. But expecting them to always be perfect is both unrealistic and unkind.

The lie of perfection can get to us in many different ways.

It might be distorting your understanding of your unique beauty. It's possibly already doing some damage to how you experience your worth. But for certain, the lie of perfection is probably also taking regular hits at your identity as a follower of Jesus. The cry I hear most from women who love Jesus is, 'I'm such a mess. I'm not a good Christian. I'm not good enough to be of any use to God.'

You might want to write down what the lie of perfection says to you. It might help to start by completing this sentence:

'I should be more . . .'

Once you've done this, speak back to the lie:

'I might not be as . . . as I would like/think I should be. But my life is hidden in Christ. So anything that needs to be worked on for my good and his glory, I give him permission to do, so you can pipe down!'

2. Stop colluding with the lie

Your thoughts are powerful.

God created you as a thinking being. You think all day long and when you fall asleep, your brain sorts through your thoughts. But instead of this happening in your brain, somehow separate from you, your thoughts are in your control. None of us can determine the thoughts that will enter our consciousness, but we do have choices around what we do with them and how we might respond. We can nurture that thought or allow it to pass on, like a train leaving a station.

Just because you think something, doesn't mean you have to do it or agree with it. You are not a victim of your thoughts. You can literally change the pathways in your brain by choosing to think differently!

This might all sound a little odd. I'm no neuroscientist, so I approach this kind of heavyweight stuff with caution. But the more I discover about how God has made my brain for harmony and connection, the more sure I am that the thoughtless way I ignore the workings of my mind leaves me wide open to repeating behaviours and feeding attitudes that hurt my mind *and* body.

It's life changing to realise that our thoughts don't have to be in charge of our lives. I can take every thought to court! I can quiz it, question it, doubt it and ultimately discard it if I don't believe it's in line with God's character and will in my life. I don't need to collude with a lie.

You can catch the negative thoughts like 'I will never be good enough'. You do this by first paying attention to what thoughts come into your brain. Ask yourself, 'Is this true?' 'Is this helpful?' 'Is this kind?' If the answer is no, then you can just let it go.

Question: 'What negative thoughts are swirling around in my brain?'

Try 'catching' them and writing them down. As far as you can, don't pass judgement on how long the list is. Longer doesn't mean you're a bad person! It just means you're being honest.

Question: 'What feelings are linked to this negative thought?'

Try and zone in on the consequences this thought has on your emotions and in your body. You could draw a larger circle around the thought and in it write the emotions and physical feelings that accompany it.

Question: 'If I kept believing this negative thought, where might it take me?'

You could draw lines from the circle to represent possible destinations for persistently thinking and believing this thought.

Question: 'Do I want to keep this negative thought in my mind, or discard it?'

You can choose whether to keep feeding this thought with your attention and emotional energy, or let it jog on!

You're going to need to persevere over time to benefit from this technique. But don't give up at the first hurdle!

3. Replace the lie

When we allow ourselves to think a thought, we're also opening ourselves up to feeling whatever emotion is attached to it, so it matters that we replace the lie – with all the discontent and shame that's attached to it – with the truth that brings life, hope and trust in God.

Being able to think is astonishing!

Being able to *choose* what to think is a miracle!

I don't mean the random thoughts that pop into your mind like 'Eat pink bananas'. I mean the power you have over what to do with the thoughts you think. For the apostle Paul, taking hold of our thoughts enables us to fully embrace the way of life Jesus models for us to copy: one of compete surrender and obedience to the will of the Father.

> 'Summing it all up, friends, I'd say you'll do best by filling your minds and meditating on things true, noble, reputable, authentic, compelling, gracious – the best, not the worst; the beautiful, not the ugly; things to praise, not things to curse. Put into practice what you learned from me, what you heard and saw and realized. Do that, and God, who makes everything work together, will work you into his most excellent harmonies.'
>
> Philippians 4:8–9, *The Message*

So maybe it's time to work on some truths to store in your mind for when you need to replace the lies. Here are some that I have set aside.

'I will use my search for happiness to inspire me to lean more on God, as he is the only one who can provide the satisfaction I crave.'

'When I feel the pull to be perfect, I will ask God to continue the work he has started in me to make me more like his son in character and obedience.'

'It's not a good idea to plan out the next ten years of my life when I'm feeling hungry, angry, lonely, tired or at 2 a.m.'

To coin a popular phrase, this is 'my truth', and in the power of the Spirit, I'm going to live it.

4. Be God's, not just good

I know I've conveniently dodged this up until now, but the fact remains that in Scripture we are told to be perfect. Well, holy to be exact. Here are two of the key passages we jump to when we're talking about the way we're called to live. 'You must be holy because I, the LORD, am holy. I have set you apart from all other people to be my very own' (Leviticus 20:26, NLT), and 'for it is written, "Be holy, because I am holy"' (1 Peter 1:16, NIV).

What does this make you think of? What does holiness look like?

Someone who's better than everyone else and knows it?

Someone who is always one step removed from real life, as if they've found a 'float-above-it' button?

A missionary? A disapproving, unfashionable one.

Holiness is problematic. St Augustine famously said, 'Lord, make me holy, but not yet.' It feels like we're about to lose something unique about us as we step into the chlorine bath of Christian holiness. Isn't it yet another way that the perfection illusion gets dumped especially onto women of faith who know that they should be being 'good girls'?

Holiness is problematic if we think of it along the lines of the false reality of self-made-happiness-promising perfection we're choosing to resist. So how else could we view it? It's important that we allow Scripture to interpret Scripture. In the Hebrew language, holiness means being set apart. So what does God mean when he entreats us to be holy?

It's a statement of identity. We belong to God who is perfect and complete. There's no sin or flaw in him. He is whole, so in belonging to him, his wholeness becomes our wholeness. When God tells his people to be holy, he's reminding them that they have been drawn into a unique relationship with him that will change everything about their identity and lifestyle. It *is* about being good, but more than anything, it's about being *God's*.

Peter picks up this command in one of his letters. But look at how he sets the context for it. It's an invitation to life.

'So roll up your sleeves, put your mind in gear, be totally
ready to receive the gift that's coming when Jesus arrives.
Don't lazily slip back into those old grooves of evil, doing
just what you feel like doing. You didn't know any better
then; you do now. As obedient children, let yourselves be
pulled into a way of life shaped by God's life, a life ener-
getic and blazing with holiness. God said, "I am holy;
you be holy" '

1 Peter 1:13–16, *The Message*

We're not being asked to do or be anything that the Father
can't or won't do in us. When we respond to this invitation to be wholly his, we're putting ourselves in the hands
of the Potter who knows how to shape the most breathtaking sculpture out of the clay in his hands.

Being God's means we can't be 'perfection'-chasers
any more. Instead, we become treasure-hunters, choosing
to invite the Spirit to do the deep work within us that
makes us more like Jesus. That perfects us in *his* perfect
love. We replace the pursuit of human perfection, which
is steeped in control, fear and the uncertainty of whether
God is enough, with openness, which is built on honesty,
obedience and trust in a God who loves us in our
fragility.

Why would we want to be chasing anything that Jesus
doesn't dream for us?

Why would we be open to anything other than the life
Jesus has for us?

It's time to discard those twisted self-expectations and
impossible goals that are holding you back from the life
you've always wanted to live. Although this is going to

be a process, you know that God is more invested in fulfilling your life than you could ever be.

Move over, Barbie. I've got my eyes on a greater prize!

'Those things were important to me, but now I think they are worth nothing because of Christ . . . I do not mean that I am already as God wants me to be. I have not yet reached that goal, but I continue trying to reach it and to make it mine. Christ wants me to do that, which is the reason he made me his. Brothers and sisters, I know that I have not yet reached that goal, but there is one thing I always do. Forgetting the past and straining toward what is ahead, I keep trying to reach the goal and get the prize for which God called me through Christ to the life above.'

Philippians 3:7, 12–14, NCV

De-construct me

Have you found yourself blaming others for your life not being as you would have hoped? Why do you think you've been doing this? Think about what it might be like if you stayed in this rut of blaming other people for the unhappiness or restlessness you feel.

Jesus never fulfils our false hopes. He won't. Not because he's cruel and uncaring, but because it wouldn't bring us the peace and fulfilment we're made to know. It might help you to name some of the false hopes about God you want to lay down. Here are some that I've had to learn to leave behind to help get you started:

God will always make me happy.
God will do what I ask him to.
Life should be fair.
God owes me the desires of my heart.

Re-construct me

If God isn't interested in fulfilling your false hopes, what *does* he promise to do? The answer is simple: he promises to bless you. The word that's mostly used for 'blessing' in the Bible is the Hebrew verb *barak*, which means to kneel as both a sign of respect, and also to receive something (as in Genesis 12:2). When God blesses us, he pours into our lives the power and resources to do what is impossible for us to do in our own strength.

I'm not going to list all the blessings in the Bible for you – they would take too many pages to list! Why don't you set yourself the goal of mining the Bible for the blessings God has promised to give you as you continue to grow in love and commitment to him? Here's a beautiful blessing about all that God has the power to do in our lives:

'There has never been the slightest doubt in my mind that the God who started this great work in you would keep at it and bring it to a flourishing finish on the very day Christ Jesus appears.'

Philippians 1:6, *The Message*

6.

MYSTERY

I was late for the flight but as there were no queues at duty free I rushed in to buy some perfume. That's when Mikel spotted me. Passionate about perfumes and certain that women should *not* be left to the enormous task of choosing their own, he took control of the situation.

'You don't want that one, madam,' he said condescendingly as he manoeuvred me away from the buy-one-get-one-free section. 'I will help you choose the perfume that is perfect for you!'

'That's OK,' I smiled sweetly. 'I've got the one I wanted, thanks.'

He obviously wasn't impressed by my choice. 'But madam, perfume is so important. It tells people who you are. It reveals your true essence!' he insisted.

'I just want this one. It's . . .'

'I know what I'm talking about,' he interrupted with a steely glint in his eye, 'and that one will not help people to know your true essence!'

I can't actually remember what I said in response, but I like to think it went something like this: 'You might be right, Mikel, but my budget can't cope with people sniffing my true essence, so I'll settle for this!' In reality I probably just mumbled an embarrassed apology as I ran to the till with my knock-down purchase.

Mikel was right about the cheap tat I'd bought – it truly stank and made no one any the wiser about my essence – but I'm not sure if the truth of an individual can be boiled down to a bottle of perfume. Aren't we more complicated than that? But maybe being complicated is why we crave simple definition, and why pretentious perfume adverts seem to work on us. There's something about a gorgeous celebrity draped in feathers and faffing around a construction site in stilettos that makes us cave to the power of the perfume! I'm all for saving money and embracing my natural state, but in the end if the choice is between a slightly expensive eau-de-gorgeous-woman or my own eau-de-BO I know I'll be choosing the former.

Essence

It's interesting to think about what we discover when we boil something down to its essential nature, but can you do that with God? We're talking about the Almighty, the one who calls himself the beginning and the end of all things. It's not easy to boil the divine down to one easy-to-grasp ingredient. But that doesn't stop us from trying!

Part of God's essence, though, is definitely *mystery*. It's core to who he is. Mysteries are those things we find difficult to grasp or impossible to get our heads round. Some men in their two-dimensional wisdom refer to women as a mystery. I used to find this charming; now it sticks in my throat. It's often cloaked in a veneer of self-deprecation: 'Ladies, be nice to us men. You're all a mystery to us because we're so stupid!' when in fact they're really implying that women are a problem to be solved (or attempting to abdicate responsibility for their own poor behaviour). The truth is that people in general are a mystery. We don't always understand ourselves and we certainly don't always understand each other.

Imagine waking up one morning and finding yourself in a tent (my worst nightmare). Tentatively you unzip the opening and see that you're halfway up a mountain in the middle of nowhere. Two questions would immediately spring to mind: 'Where am I?' and 'How did I get here?' It would be impossible to know what to do until you had these two answers nailed.

On a cosmic level we're asking the same two questions. Our existence is a mystery. Look at the tips of your fingers. The chances of anyone having the exact same finger print as you is *one in sixty-four billion*. You have a unique combination of experiences, hopes, skills and personality traits. You may live in a world that tells you you're here by chance, but *everything* points to your existence as being nothing short of an utter miracle.

You are fearfully and wonderfully made.

The mystery of our own existence is wrapped up in the mystery of the one who made us. Part of the beautiful essence of God is his mystery – he is closer to us than our skin, yet he is outside time and space. He is the lion and the lamb, the victorious warrior and the willing sacrifice. Our limited knowledge of his holiness and yet our experience of his comforting love can leave us struggling to fathom who he is. David captures this brilliantly in one of his psalms:

'In my distress I screamed to the Lord for his help. And he heard me from heaven; my cry reached his ears. Then the earth rocked and reeled, and mountains shook and trembled. How they quaked! For he was angry. Fierce flames leaped from his mouth, setting fire to the earth; smoke blew from his nostrils. He bent the heavens down and came to my defense; thick darkness was beneath his feet. Mounted on a mighty angel, he sped swiftly to my aid with wings of wind. He enshrouded himself with darkness, veiling his approach with dense clouds dark as murky waters. Suddenly the brilliance of his presence broke through the clouds with lightning and a mighty storm of hail.'

Psalm 18:6–12, TLB

This is God, who is terrifying in his power and yet swift to come to our rescue. He's always beyond us, hard to glimpse and often out of reach. Even when we feel God is close, he doesn't always behave how we think he should. I remember a friend weeping into my lap one Sunday evening at church. She was tired of the feeling of walking through a thick cloud with God completely hidden from her. 'Why doesn't he reveal himself to me?' she kept asking. 'If I were God I'd have shown up by now!'

I completely understood her ache. It's hard to walk in the company of a God who is so often clouded in mystery. How many times I have shouted into the sky or into my pillow, 'Where are you, God?' Those times we cry out to him and hear nothing in return but the sound of silence can feel like a betrayal. Why doesn't he do what I'm longing for? How can he stand by and do nothing? I don't get it! But if this were a God I could fathom with my mind, would I still see him as God? If I could contain him, would I *want* him? This is where we touch the limitations of our minds because there's something about God's mystery that, although formidable, is truly comforting. Then again, how can I find comfort from a God I can't ever fully know?

I suppose the answer is simple – because he is all-powerful and he is all-loving. The two are perfectly combined, which means I can trust him to do what's right, even if I don't understand what he's doing. The simple conundrum is this: if we could completely understand God, *we* would be God. If he acted according to our plans, he would be *us*. What's left is a choice. Do we hold on to our expectations of a God we think we know, or let go of our finite ideas and begin to find him?

Wild goose

Ancient Celtic Christians abandoned their limitations of God. These early crazy missionaries, who set off on the wild seas in tiny boats from places like Ireland to bring faith to the rest of the British Isles, didn't want to constrain God. Their own encounters with the Spirit and what they read in Scripture told them that God was bigger than they could grasp. They couldn't bend him to their will or force his hand. He was a wild God, as unpredictable as the seas they set out on. How could the God who held the depth of the ocean in his hands and commanded the storms to be stilled with one word, be controlled by the people he had made?

So they chose to depict the Holy Spirit as a wild goose; a bird that is strong, undomesticated and impossible to contain.

When I was a teenager I heard geese most nights, honking as they flew in formation over our house. By then we had moved to live with the community at Ashburnham Place where the geese were a fixture of life. There's nothing particularly safe or reassuring about these birds. They've got a noisy honk and can knock you over if you get too close! But the Celtic Church saw something in these wild geese that spoke to them of a God they couldn't bend to their will.

Wild God.

Mysterious God.

Is this how you experience God?

Time and again we see in Scripture a God who cannot be tamed or trapped. In the Gospels we read of Jesus healing the outcast and upturning tables at a market in the Temple. He dismantles people's false expectations of who the Messiah should be and fulfils broken hopes. He singles out the poor in spirit as inheritors of his kingdom. He invites the weak, the broken and the dispossessed as well as the religious and the rich to follow him. He sends out his uneducated and volatile disciples to cast out demons and heal the sick. He calms storms on lakes and whips up storms in the hearts of those who want to silence the things of God.

This is what the Celts experienced; a God who wasn't to be subdued, but pursued. Over oceans if that's where they needed to go. One of the most famous of the Celtic saints, St Brendan, set out from Ireland in his little boat on a legendary voyage to North America. I can imagine him kneeling on the beach and looking out at the wide expanse of the ocean, whispering;

> 'Help me to journey beyond the familiar
> and into the unknown.
> Give me the faith to leave old ways
> and break fresh ground with You.
> Christ of the mysteries, I trust You
> to be stronger than each storm within me.
> I will trust in the darkness and know
> that my times, even now, are in Your hand.
> Tune my spirit to the music of heaven,
> and somehow, make my obedience count for You.'
>
> Prayer of St Brendan (484–577)[1]

What strikes me in reading some of the prayers written by the Celtic Church at this time is that even though they knew God to be wild, he wasn't a stranger. They knew his intimate presence in the best and also the darkest of times. He wasn't a distant star they were following; he was closer than their breath. He travelled with them in the boats. They knew without a doubt that this is a God who wants to be known by us and that the greatest unfolding in our lives happens as we go deeper into the mystery of who God is.

Unfold

In all our relationships with people there's an element of both the known and the unknown, certainty and uncertainty.

You could say that a six-month-old baby knows its mother intimately. But on another level they know *nothing* about the mum or who she is. But that's OK, because it's a growing relationship. Think about your closest friend. For all you know about them, there are bound to be things you don't know. But this doesn't stop you wanting to know them better. In fact, it drives you forward to knowing them more. Even couples who have been married for many years talk about how their loved one is still a mystery to them. A wonderful mystery, but a mystery nonetheless. We are mysterious creatures, created to unfurl in our relationships with the people we're most intimate with.

Relationships are made to grow, but they don't grow automatically. Growth requires vulnerability, vulnerability requires intimacy and intimacy requires commitment. That's how God has designed it. Contemporary dating culture puts forward the idea that everything can happen between two people before a commitment is made, but God's idea is the other way around. The commitment to be exclusive and faithful to each other is a green light for the vulnerability and intimacy to be released that permits growth. This is why I encourage people to not have sex in a relationship until a commitment of exclusivity is made before God, because sex always brings the possibility of *more* into a relationship. It's an act of the soul, not just the body, that is designed to bond two people into one flesh. I think that delaying sex is a way of honouring the potential we all have to lose ourselves into another person. A couple who have created a bond before God of exclusive, faithful and committed love are releasing sexual intimacy to be the source of satisfaction, strength and comfort for their relationship that God designed it to be.

We are made to slowly unfold into each other, learning the mysteries of each other as we go.

It's exactly the same with God. You can unfold into God. You can throw yourself with abandon into exploring who he is because he is already utterly committed to you. The key is to learn to listen to him. That in itself is a mystery.

So how is it that we can hear God's voice? Well, to put it simply, because he wants us to! All relationships rely on communication to grow. With your friend or partner it might be obvious when they are trying to tell you something. Being a bit of an eye-contact junkie I get so frustrated when my husband doesn't look at me when I'm talking to him! Paying attention to what the other person is saying and *meaning* is essential to true communication. The more we learn to recognise when God is speaking to us, the more we will grow in knowledge of him and intimacy with him. Jesus not only speaks the words of God, he *is* the Word of God. He is the living, breathing mystery of God. We hear the voice of Jesus as we read Scripture.

Listen

When Jesus was baptised by his cousin John, the Holy Spirit came to settle on his head in the form of a dove, and the Father spoke over him, '"This is my Son, whom I have chosen; listen to him"' (Luke 9:35, NIV). The Father doesn't say, 'Chat about him', or 'Make notes on great sermons about him' or even 'Talk to him', but '*Listen* to him'. It's so important that the Father repeats it again when Jesus takes his closest friends up the mountain. 'But while he was still speaking these words, a cloud covered them, blotting out the sun, and a voice from the cloud said, "*This* is my beloved Son. Listen to *him*"' (Mark 9:7, TLB).

God is inviting us to listen to Jesus. It must be because there are things he wants us to hear!

A great place to start is in the Gospels, the accounts of Christ's life and teachings from the people who were there with him. I love poring over the encounters Jesus has with people. He's so tender with people that others have rejected (John 4:1–42) and he's so firm with people who think they know what God is all about (Matthew 23:13). Here's how you can listen out for the voice of Jesus as you read the Bible.

Choose a Jesus story in Scripture that piques your curiosity.

1. Ask Jesus to help you hear his voice as you read it.

2. Read the passage slowly.

3. Let your mind wander around the story, thinking about what you've read, words or phrases that strike you, and the things you're curious about. *Why did she say that? What does that mean?* Ask Jesus to speak to you as you read it again.

4. Read the passage again.

5. Ask yourself, 'What can I hear Jesus saying to me as I read this story?'

6. Read the passage one final time.

7. Try and capture in a sentence what Jesus is saying to you.

You might be wondering how you know if the thoughts you have are from God or just your brilliant mind! Well, God never contradicts himself. He won't tell you something that is against his character. So if you have the thought that God hates a certain group of people, you can rule that out – it's not God's voice. Psalm 145:9 tells us that God has compassion on all he has made and John 3:16 tells us that God sent Jesus because he loves everyone and everything in his creation. So if you feel you hear God saying something that you're not sure about, take it to the Bible and see if it contradicts something that he has said elsewhere, and ask others who are mature in their faith whether they think it's God's voice or your own ideas.

As you tune your mind into hearing the voice of Jesus, you will grow in confidence, recognising his voice among the chatter in your mind. I find that God speaks to me as I'm reading a passage of Scripture by dropping into my mind a clear thought about who he is or who I am. It might be as simple as 'I am loved by God'. Of course, I also have thoughts about what I'll be eating for dinner and why so and so hasn't messaged me back! But then I just draw my mind back to the passage and remain open to God bringing a thought into my mind that makes me think about him in more depth. The more I do this, the more I've come to recognise whether that's Jesus' voice or not.

The other way we can listen is by being open to God's voice in our everyday lives through other people, impressions we get about things and experiences we go through. I think that Jesus loves to confirm his word through a whole range of ways. He's God, he can speak to us however he wants to! There have been times when someone has sent me a text with a word or thought that has pressed home the truth of what I heard Jesus say to me earlier when I was reading the Bible. We all have a unique psyche that God knows intimately – so he may well choose to speak to you very differently from how he chooses to speak to me. Even if he wants to say the same thing!

Remember that the *whole* of the Bible is inspired by God, which means that you can hear the voice of Jesus every time you read Scripture. 'There's nothing like the written Word of God for showing you the way to salvation through faith in Christ Jesus. Every part of Scripture is God-breathed and useful one way or another—showing us truth, exposing our rebellion, correcting our mistakes, training us to live God's way. Through the Word we are put together and shaped up for the tasks God has for us' (2 Timothy 3:16–17, *The Message*). Jesus is speaking to you through every word, every story, every random list, psalm or historical account. It is all the Word of God so get ready to hear Jesus speaking to you every time you read or listen to God's Word.

If that's not an incredible mystery, I don't know what is!

If reading the Bible for ourselves enables us to better explore the mystery of God, why don't we do it? Well, for starters we're busy and easily distracted, and secondly the Bible is a hard book to read. It's actually an expansive collection of books (plural) with everything from lists of people whose names we can't pronounce and instructions for building a temple in a wilderness to laws that go into excruciating detail, letters to persecuted Christians and stories of war and suffering perpetrated by the people of God. But here's the thing: if we know that God wants to speak to us as we read his word, we can approach everything we read in the Bible with a fresh expectation that God wants to reveal himself to us. Just like the little boy Samuel in the Temple who wasn't sure whose voice he was hearing calling him in the night, we can dare to say, 'Speak, Lord. I am your servant and I am listening' (1 Samuel 3:11, NCV).

But we don't just listen to know more. We listen to obey.

I'm sure I'm not the only one who feels I have a supernatural fight on my hands when I have made the decision to read my Bible more. I think the enemy fights us so hard when we're about to open our Bibles because he knows that listening to Jesus and obeying what he says to us makes us a threat to him. He doesn't know God's specific plans for our lives, but he knows Scripture. He knows that ultimately he is defeated and we are free. But he also knows that if he can fill our minds with uncertainty about our identity and keep us from the very book that would help us to listen to who we are in Jesus, he can get us living in defeat and fear.

I've met a number of women who are unsure that God has anything specific to say to them. Sometimes it's because they think that only people who have a PhD in studying the Bible are allowed to hear from God. The problem with this false belief is that it encourages us to take the things that other people say as the absolute word of God without checking it for ourselves. Some churches and Christian teachers rely on people only wanting to hear God second-hand, so that they can push forward their own toxic ideas about who is or isn't loved by God.

Have you got used to expecting a kind of spiritual hand-me-down experience of hearing God's voice?

My entire early teenage wardrobe was made up of hand-me-downs. Generous friends with older daughters bagged up stuff they didn't need any more. I loved them but the clothes weren't really *me*. Though I do think it fuelled my passion for shopping in second-hand shops today. But when I turned sixteen I was taken to buy a pair of oxblood Dr. Martens boots. I felt I had stepped over the threshold of a different world, and I wasn't going back! I remember it so vividly. *This is what it feels like to wear stuff that fits me!* I thought.

Jesus wants to speak to you, and Jesus *is* speaking to you.

Every promise in Scripture is *yours* because Jesus has fulfilled everything required for you to inherit it. These promises of hope for a life in all its fullness now and in the life to come have been given to you by Jesus. 'I am holding you by your right hand—I, the Lord your God—

and I say to you, Don't be afraid; I am here to help you' (Isaiah 41:13, TLB). You're not receiving blessings that have been made for others and passed on to you as an afterthought. Every word of life that comes from the heart of God is fresh for you, new every morning.

I want to encourage you to fight for your times alone with Scripture. To grab your Bible (a physical copy, a digital one or perhaps an audio version) and treasure it as it reveals to you the mysteries of God's character and mission. To find moments to get familiar with the stories you love and wrestle with the passages you struggle to understand. The Word of God in your hands and Jesus, the Word of God who takes your thoughts captive and speaks to you in your mind, will arm you when the lies of the enemy murmur that you are not worthy to be loved by God.

Reach out

But as well as us listening to God, the truth is that God is listening to *you*. Imagine that – the greatest mystery in the entire universe is turning his ear towards you.

I think that prayer is best explained as us reaching out to God. Often we think of prayer as well-crafted sentences that sound important and are said by people who are given permission by other seemingly important people to speak to God. I love hearing ancient prayers, used by people who love the wonder of words which have been uttered by millions of people over hundreds of years. But some of my most intimate moments of speaking to God are experienced are when I'm at a loss for words and trip over my sentences. I don't make any sense to myself, but somehow, mysteriously, I make perfect sense to God. It's no wonder that this is the kind of prayer that the Father seems to love the most. When asked to quickly workshop how people should pray to God, Jesus responds in such a practical and down to earth way. 'Here's what I want you to do,' says Jesus to his disciples in Matthew 6:6 (*The Message*). 'Find a quiet, secluded place so you won't be tempted to role-play before God. Just be there as simply and honestly as you can manage. The focus will shift from you to God, and you will begin to sense his grace.'

If prayer isn't simple and honest, it might be a whole lot of other things, but it's not the intimate connection with the Father that Jesus invites us to practise. When we're overwhelmed by his love or when we're at the end of our rope, when we're seeking direction or when we're seeking forgiveness, scripture tells us that when we pray in the name of Jesus, our voice is heard in the throne room of heaven, the very place where God is ruling. And our deepest cries are heard by Jesus who fully understands our weaknesses and failings. He intercedes to the Father on our behalf with an insight and knowledge none of us can get our heads around.

'Now that we know what we have—Jesus, this great High Priest with ready access to God—let's not let it slip through our fingers. We don't have a priest who is out of touch with our reality. He's been through weakness and testing, experienced it all—all but the sin. So let's walk right up to him and get what he is so ready to give. Take the mercy, accept the help.'

Hebrews 4:14–16, *The Message*

But prayer is more than communicating our dreams and desires to God. Prayer is like breathing. We do it because it sustains us. Belonging to God isn't about agreeing with a set of doctrines; first and foremost it's about becoming a new person who is powered by the life-giving Spirit of God. We pray to live just as we breathe to live! And because prayer is something we can do naturally, so much teaching on prayer suggests we begin by relaxing, breathing deeply and focusing our mind on the presence of God rather than rushing in with a ready made list of things to ask God for. Prayer can be about wrestling with God over life's mysteries or shouting at him through the pain that you're experiencing, but why not begin to build it into your life with something simple?

Lisa wanted to pray out loud. But she'd only recently become a Christian and always felt too intimidated in groups of 'older' Christians to do so. She was convinced she'd get it all wrong. So we went for a walk and we chatted about her life, her dreams, her favourite film – you know the kind of things. We just nattered as we wandered along the canal near her home. The next time we met up, I suggested that she talked to God as we walked along. Just the things that we had been chatting about.

'That's weird,' she said.

'I know,' I said, 'but it'll become natural.'

So we walked and chatted, and occasionally I would say, 'Lisa, why don't you tell God that?' and she would. She didn't start with 'Dear God' or end with 'Amen'. She just walked and talked. Honestly, simply.

More recently I've had to learn how to pray simply and honestly again. Since becoming a mum I've woken up to how fragile life is, and how little we know about what will happen tomorrow – let alone in the future. One day I was reading the words of Peter who, like me, felt passion for life and also at times deep anxiety: 'Let [God] have all your worries and cares, for he is always thinking about you and watching everything that concerns you' (1 Peter 5:7, TLB), and the words 'God before Google' dropped into my mind. I realised that although I was praying regularly for others and with others, I wasn't being all that honest about the things that were really on my heart; my concern for my little girl as she grows up and my worry that I won't cope if she doesn't sleep! I was heading straight to search engines to try and reassure me that everything was going to be OK, when the truth is, no one can promise me that.

God before Google.

We live in an age when easy information (and fake news) is only a swipe or click away. Companies promise to take the wanting out of waiting and same-day delivery means nothing need be out of our reach for too long. Into this mix we are invited to know a God who is way beyond our human understanding, and yet comes to find us in the person of Jesus. As women who are being found in Christ, we are invited to find God, in all his wonder and mystery. It's the greatest pursuit. It's the wildest goose chase!

> 'My choice is you, GOD, first and only.
> And now I find I'm *your* choice!
> Now you've got my feet on the life path,
> all radiant from the shining of your face.

Ever since you took my hand,
I'm on the right way.'

Psalm 16:5, 11, *The Message*

De-construct me

Find a quiet and safe space to sit with your thoughts about who God is and your hopes for your relationship with him. Do you have broken hopes from those times you cried out to God and felt nothing but his silence and absence? Bring that to him now. When you feel ready, read these words below and use them to lead you into prayer to the God who in his mystery invites us to know him.

'Through the wisdom of God we are not left alone to face our fractured minds, but are armed with His word to test every thought that passes through our minds. Through the power of God we are not left weak – because His power is made perfect in our weakness as it reveals more of Him. Through the love of God we are strengthened, for whatever anguish we suffer we are assured that through Jesus our depths are never further than His love for us. Through the healing of God our wounds are given balm; through the touch of the physician's hand or medication's flow we can know that our minds are not abandoned to the darkness.

When the answers to our prayers feel lost in the mystery of God and when we are desperate for answers and all we can hear is silence – we are not abandoned to the darkness. We recall the tears from the darkness and point to what we hope in.

That the God for whom stars were an afterthought will lead us home and our questions will be answered at the sight of His glorious face.'

Rachael Newham, founder of ThinkTwice, a Christian mental health charity (quoted with kind permission)

Re-construct me

Imagine you're somewhere you feel safe and calm. There are two really comfortable chairs in the room, facing each other. You sit in one of them. You've taken your shoes off and are snuggled into the chair, feeling really peaceful. Jesus comes and sits in the other one. You can see just from the expression on his face that he loves you and is so happy to be with you. For a few moments you sit together in silence. Then you begin to speak to him. What do you say?

Once you've spoken out all those thoughts in your mind, sit in silence with Jesus again. Allow this verse from the Bible to roll around your mind as you sit with him in silence.

'Be still, and know that I am God.'

Psalm 46:10, NLT

Do this for a couple of minutes.

Then Jesus leans forward and begins to speak to you. Listen to him. What does he say to you?

I have a folder on my laptop called 'bucket', where I keep a record of all the things I sense God is saying to me through reading the Bible, praying or meditating or through other people. I want to encourage you to capture what you think God is saying to you. To begin with it might all feel random or insignificant. But keep going. God is speaking to you, and over time you will begin to see building up in your folder or journal a long list of the things God is drawing to your attention to build you up, inspire you and equip you for the life he is giving you.

SOUL.

'The soul, fortunately, has an interpreter – often an unconscious but still a faithful interpreter – in the eye.'

Charlotte Bronte, *Jane Eyre*

'For God alone my soul waits in silence;
from him comes my salvation.'

Psalm 62:1, ESV

7.

PAUSE

You were made for adventure.

To feel the wind in your face. To choose a place on a map and go there! To get some scrapes and bruises as you climb a tree. To gaze at horizons, light fires in wild places and sleep out in the open.

OK. Maybe scaling the Himalayas before dinner is a little unrealistic. For some of us, our capacity for adventure might look more like the art we create rather than the mountains we climb, but the fact remains that you and I were made for more than viewing life through a screen or experiencing everything second-hand. As great as digital technologies and the latest comforts are, you are made for something richer than modern life can offer you. You are made to *really* live.

So when was the last time that you did something for the *first* time? When did you last go on an adventure?

Life is an adventure. Being alive is a complete miracle. But it doesn't always feel like an adventure. That's not because we're not brave (or wealthy) enough to book the flights to go white-water rafting down the Zambezi River. It's because we don't stand still enough. I know that sounds like a total contradiction, but life doesn't always feel like an adventure because we don't take time out from the endless buzz of input that the digital age surrounds us with. There is intense demand on us all the time to stay focused and in control – to do life in a set way. There's a relentless compulsion to be on top of our lives and successful in everything we do. Modern technology makes sure that we're always 'on', always reachable by our boss or peers, always glued to people's opinions of us on our screens.

'The developers of apps and games and social media sites are dedicated to trapping us in what are called ludic loops. These are short cycles of repeated actions which feed our brain's desire for reward. Every point you score, every candy you crush, every retweet you get gives your brain a dopamine hit that keeps you coming back for more. You're not having a bit of harmless fun: you are an addict. A tech corporation has taken your solitude and monetised it. It's not the game that is being played – it's you.'

Paul Kingsnorth, writing in *New Statesman*[1]

But this isn't the life you and I were made to know. We are made for more. For *adventure*.

So how can doing nothing be the beginning of an adventure?

Well, adventures are nothing if not challenging. You don't wander out to the corner shop for a late night chocolate bar and call it an adventure. An adventure requires you to flex some muscles you didn't know you had and step out of your comfort zone to find what might lie on the other side of your fear! But I wonder if our greatest adventure isn't waiting for us 'out there', but 'in here'. Could it be that the life we're longing for can only be found when we stop?

There's nothing more terrifying than silence. I'm talking about the total absence of people telling us what to think, advertisers telling us what to buy, companies telling us what to do, the media telling us who to be. Without all this input, who are we?

And yet there's no God-given resource that we're more in need of in our lives today than pressing pause, turning down the dial and choosing silence. Why? Because silence creates space in us to find who we are. By choosing moments of silence (no phones, no screens, no Spotify playing in the background) we're opening ourselves up to the possibility that our lives could feel and be different.

Stopping, waiting, pausing – none of this comes easy! As an extrovert activist I'm constantly looking for life in the fast lane. I love the thrill of a new project. I love visiting new places, meeting different people, learning new things. If something needs to be done, let me do it! I know, I'm a nightmare. Even crossing the road I'm the person who darts between cars because I haven't got time to hang around for a little green guy to decide to show up. I remember once at university hiding in the wardrobe of a guy I fancied, so that I could jump out and surprise him when he came back from his lecture. I was one classy lady! After waiting for what felt like an age (at least five minutes) I climbed back out of the window to go and find someone else to jump out at.

A few years later I found myself running a youth charity, and I loved it. There were always decisions to be made, people to network with, young people to reach. It was a job that was never done. There was always more to do. After a while I found that I was working round the clock and every weekend to try and stay one step ahead. After a few years of me turning into Wifezilla whenever I had to stop work for a mini-vacation, my husband and I decided that for the benefit of our holiday and protection of our marriage, there would be one day where Jason would head into the hills and do whatever he does out in the wilds alone, and I would mope around annoying no one but myself. Jason loved the space to be alone – I hated it! I felt trapped with the one person (me) whose company I liked the least, so I'd sneak out into the nearby town and distract myself with endless shopping or chatting at unsuspecting pensioners.

While holidaying in the Lake District one year, I found myself chatting to some elderly men at a bus stop who were waiting for the coach to take them on their day trip. They had a free space as poor Enid's knees were playing her up. As my knees were in good working order, I jumped on the coach and had a brilliant day with a bunch of octogenarians! But for all the fun times with random strangers, the truth was that I was struggling to be still and face myself. Like many other people in our hooked-up, switched-on culture, I knew that the moment I shut the door, switched off the screens and turned off my phone it would just be me, myself and I – and that made me afraid. I didn't want to hear the agitated voice of my ego telling me that I was missing out and I couldn't afford to stop. I was terrified of opportunities passing me by. It was ridiculous and it was exhausting. It still is sometimes. But I'm learning to do something life-changing on a regular basis.

I'm learning to pause. To take the chance in the midst of a hectic life to . . .

Stop.

Break off.

Take a break.

Take a breath.

Take a moment.

Wait.

Pull up.

Pull back.

Mark time.

Create space.

Rest.

Inhale.

Interrupt.

Slow down.

Wind down.

What from that list jumps out at you? Read it again.

You don't need to be a raging extrovert like me to need to press the pause button once in a while. In the twenty-first century our brains are trained to think in fast-forward. We're always looking for the next message, the next Instagram pic, the next game, the next film, the next latest greatest cat-caught-in-a-tumble-dryer clip on You-Tube. It can be impossible to find silence. There's always something flashing and beeping at us, crying out for our attention. Even writing this I'm checking a social media thread, work emails and my online bank account! In fact sometimes it doesn't just feel as if we're living stuck in fast-forward, sometimes it feels as if we're stuck in the middle of a data tornado. Why don't we switch off, shut it down, pull out, go off the grid, walk away, wait a few seconds before responding? Maybe we don't even realise we have a choice anymore. Or maybe it's more profound. Maybe we fear missing out and being isolated in a world that moves on rapidly without us. How many of us would be brave enough to admit that even with our busy lives and all our 'friends' on social media, we're often lonely?

'Loneliness among young people is a problem that has been slowly uncovered in polls. Eighty-six per cent of millennials reported feeling lonely and depressed in a 2011 study. A study in 2014 found 18–24-year-olds were four times as likely to feel lonely all the time as those aged 70 and above.'

Heather Saul, *The Independent*[2]

I don't think we have any fewer *real* friendships today than previous generations did. The issue is more to do with the exaggeration of belonging that oozes out of social media. It sets ridiculously high expectations on the amount of close contact we think we should have with people to feel that we belong. We look at someone's Instagram account and wonder why our social life is nothing like theirs. The chances are that *their* social life looks nothing like that either! But if we think that everyone else is always having the best time with great people and all we've done this week is watch a movie with our flatmate, we can feel like a social outcast. Social media filters are designed to give life a glow that isn't really there. To give the impression of adventure in the ordinary.

Instagram your pot noodle with the message 'Best night out with the girls ever!' and I *guarantee* someone somewhere will feel that their life doesn't live up to yours.

So how do we handle our loneliness and the false expectations that feed our sense of isolation? How do we give our fear of missing out a good kicking? How do we discover how to really, truly live?

The answer is simple. So back to our little mantra for this chapter – we need to learn to find ways to . . .

Stop.
Break off.
Take a break.
Take a breath.
Take a moment.
Wait.
Pull up.
Pull back.
Mark time.
Create space.
Rest.
Inhale.
Interrupt.
Slow down.
Wind down.

To reconnect with our soul.

By choosing to pause, we're daring to believe there might be a voice we're drowning out in the cacophony of sound that fills our lives. You're probably busy with a whole heap of hurry and worry in your life. You don't want to let people down and don't want to miss out, but you cannot possibly stay in the loop and keep everyone happy all the time. You might look like a graceful swan on the outside, gliding calmly across the pond of life, but underneath your little legs are powering hard to keep yourself afloat! I'm not telling you to get out of the pond. You don't need to escape your life.

You just need to listen to the voice inside that needs to be heard. It's the voice of your soul.

Time to stop

It's hard to define what we mean by soul. It isn't a floaty, ethereal thing and it isn't a *part* of you; it *is* you. You're more than flesh and bones, you're soul. In 1892, children's author and theologian George Macdonald wrote, 'We don't have a soul, we are a soul. We have a body.' We read in Genesis that the body isn't a soul-cage; God didn't make a body and then shove a soul inside. Instead he took the dust of the ground and by breathing onto it made it a soul. Scripture tells us that a soul is a being that can move and connect, dream, laugh, eat and hope. We *are* soul. Our body 'gives flesh and bone expression to our soul' (Brian Draper). The old King James version of the Bible puts it brilliantly: 'And the LORD God formed man of the dust of the ground, and breathed into his nostrils the breath of life; and man became a living soul' (Genesis 2:7).

I love how the Bible turns the tables on how modern life views humanity. We're often told we're little more than animals who live by our instincts. What a horrible way to approach the mysterious depths that lie within each one of us! Our bodies give expression to the place where we connect on the deepest level with who God is and who we are. Our minds form the language to articulate who we are and the cry of longing deep within our soul. When we pause to experience rest with God, we discover that we are more than just a mind and a body; we are a powerful, beautiful soul.

This is why pressing pause is the key to feeling alive! Because it's when we choose to be still with God that he takes us into the adventure of knowing ourselves more.

Time for a little soul exploration. For this, you'll need to not just read the next bit, but dare to do it!

Pause to listen

Being still is the main way we hear God's voice. In fact, we get the feeling from Scripture that this is God's preferred way to speak to us. He can reveal himself through the fire and the mighty thunder, but it's when we're still that we experience the still small voice of God breathing life into our soul.

> 'Be still, and know that I am God . . .'
>
> Psalm 46:10, NIV

You can be still.

Here, now.

Find a place where you feel comfortable to sit or lie down. Take a few deep breaths. It's funny, isn't it? We breathe all the time without thinking, but the moment we focus on our breathing we realise we have this incredible

God-given ability to slow ourselves down and calm our mind and body and connect with our soul. Simply by breathing deeply.

Breathe in.

Breathe out.

Breathe in. Hold it.

Breathe out.

Now, for a few minutes, allow yourself to be still. Don't worry about the random thoughts or the strange sounds your stomach makes! Allow yourself to notice your thoughts and feelings, but don't focus your energy and attention on them.

(. . . space for you to be still . . .)

How was that?

Give yourself some time to process being still.

You might be a pro at all this! Or, like me, you might have found that hard.

I'd like to invite you to do it again. But this time, invite your soul to speak. Remember, you *are* soul. I'm not talking about tuning in to your alter ego or imaginary friend! I'm encouraging you to let the real you in you connect with the God who made you and loves you like no other. So this time, as you sit in stillness, welcome God into your soul. Invite him to find you at the core of who you are. As you do, you'll become aware that God is also welcoming you into *his* presence.

You might like to repeat these words a few times: 'For God alone my soul waits in silence' (Psalm 62:1, ESV).

(. . . space for you to be still . . .)

How was that?

Give yourself some time to process connecting with your soul.

I love using verses from Scripture to help me be still. I have so many random thoughts that want to invade my mind when I try to press pause. Most of it is my false self, telling me I'm an outcast and not worthy of love. When we chew on God's word we are taking deep into our soul the recognition that we are first and foremost centred in God. We find that this, our identity, roots us in any moment. Here are some great promises from Scripture:

'Draw close to God, and he will draw close to you.'

James 4:8, ESV

'The LORD will take delight in [me], and in his love he will give [me] new life.

He will sing and be joyful over [me] . . .'

Zephaniah 3:17, GNB

'I've never quit loving you and never will. Expect love, love and more love.'

Jeremiah 31:3–4, *The Message*

'This is what the LORD says: "Stand at the crossroads and look; ask for the ancient paths, ask where the good way is, and walk in it, and you will find rest for your souls."'

Jeremiah 6:16, NIV

We need to hear God speaking over us his truth about who we are because it's the only voice that is complete in knowledge and love of us. How often does the truth of your immense value and belovedness bounce off you like a ping-pong ball? But when you pause, breathe deeply and reconnect with your soul, you give yourself the chance to receive into your being the truth that you are loved by God.

Only God knows the way around the universe that is your soul. Whenever you welcome him and listen to his voice, you find yourself in deeper ways too. 'You never know,' writes Brian Draper in his brilliant book *Soulfulness*, 'you might actually be surprised by who you really are.

We spend so much of our time trying to second-guess other people's expectations of who we should be that we get caught up in trying to fulfil all those hypothetical expectations, instead of learning more about what makes us "us".[3]

Brian's coined the word 'soulfulness' to capture a way of being that enables us to connect with our soul and the life that God is inviting us into. This doesn't mean locking ourselves away from the world – it's a daring way to live in the world. Alert to life as God sees it, ready to experience life as he designed it. When we feel the tug of our soul to pause and take in the wonder and awe of the moment, we respond, rather than rush on by to the next thing.

'True to your word,
you let me catch my breath
and send me in the right direction.'

Psalm 23:3, *The Message*

Catch my breath. Connect with my soul.

God is not just a guide to us but to the life that he's created us for. As we pause and explore the wonder of knowing that God is with us in this very moment, we might find he gently redirects our plans. He might want to draw our gaze to what *he* is looking at, not what we think is important. My friend Zoe is great at listening to her soul and allowing God to lead her to see and do things she hadn't planned for. She's amazing at texting people the messages of encouragement and hope that she feels God gives her for them. She says 'If I kept rushing by and ignoring what my soul is telling me, I wouldn't be able to hear what God wants to give me for others.'

When I sit in stillness and wait for my soul, I experience who I am made to be. I also find the space to believe that I can become that person. This is where I find the confidence to dream and take risks that lead to adventure.

So what do you dream that God could do with your life? No matter how daring your hopes are, the moment you find God in stillness, he will stir your imagination and ignite your vision in ways you could never imagine. 'The real voyage of discovery consists not in seeking new landscapes, but in having new eyes,' wrote Marcel Proust. This is the experience of the disciples, apostles, ancient saints and everyday heroines and heroes whose lives continue to touch us. They chose to see with the eyes of their soul the life of adventure that God was offering them. We stand on the shoulders of giants as we dare to pause and invite God to fill our very souls with the fire of his love.

I dare you to pause, and to never stop exploring.

De-construct me

What stops you from pressing pause? If you can, name at least three things that happen when you try to slow down or take a rest. Try not to pass judgement on what you've written. It is what it is. But it's possible for these barriers to be removed.

Bring them to God. Lay them out before him and invite

him to deal with whatever fear, insecurity, pain or unforgiveness lies at the root of these.

What helps me is to actually picture my own barriers as I bring them to God. One of mine is a fear of what my false self might say if I stop. I can hear with the ears of my soul the disapproving voices lurking outside the room I'm in. I worry that if I stop in order to be still, they will flood the room with their criticisms and judgement. So I ask God to stand guard at the door. He does. But more amazingly, he also allows me to pass through the corridor in my soul where all these voices are lurking, and know that their lies don't stick.

Re-construct me

Your soul needs space to breathe and dream. Choosing stillness is not just a great idea; it's a spiritual discipline that Scripture calls the Sabbath. In the story of the creation of the world, God worked hard for six days to form mountains and forests, birds and sea creatures – everything in the known universe and beyond. On the final day of this week of creative explosion, he sat back to enjoy all he had made.

We're humans, created in God's likeness, to live in the world he has made and notice its wonder. We don't do this when we're rushing around trying to make something of ourselves. We do it when we stop and become still. Giving yourself regular pause points allows you to expand into the richness of the life God has for you and to imagine life from his perspective. Take a moment to make some plans for pausing.

1. When is your day off? As Christians we are called to the rhythm of weekly Sabbath. It's one day in the week where we pause from producing stuff or being consumers to remind ourselves that we are made for God alone.

2. Do you have a moment each week where you do something that feeds your soul – like going for a long walk, reading a book for pleasure (not study), doing some stand-up comedy, baking, playing sport, tinkering on your car? Whatever helps you connect with your soul. If not, make one!

3. Is there a moment every day where you pause to look to God? It might be that when you wake up, you speak over yourself, 'My soul finds rest in God alone. My salvation comes from him . . .' before you check Twitter or emails.

4. Choose to see the awe and wonder of everyday moments. Notice the flowers growing in the broken cracks of the pavement, or the sunlight streaming through the window. Look people in the eyes and treat them as living souls who bear the image of God.

8.

HURT

'Baby, I'm not made of stone. It hurts.'

Emeli Sandé, 'Hurts'[1]

She's crying.

People are shifting in their seats. It's awkward to see a woman cry in this male-only space where important things such as power, politics and the finer points of the law are discussed. Of course it would be a woman who disturbs us with her tears. Then she lets her hair down! It's too much. I invited the Rabbi here so that I could work him out, not so that she could fawn all over him with her expensive perfume and loose morals. If he was the man he said he was, he'd know who was touching him and the kind of woman she is.

'I know her.' His eyes meet mine across the table. 'But it's not me who's failed the test, Simon. It's you. She's shown more respect to my feet than you've shown to my face.'

The account of the wordless woman anointing Jesus' feet with her tears and drying them with her hair is iconic. You may have seen depictions of this story in paintings or murals. Art helps the poignancy of a moment come alive, allowing us to visualise what happened. Which matters, because what happened was so significant and central to our understanding of who Jesus is and what he does that all the Gospel writers include a version of this story. He's God himself, who receives and embraces us in our brokenness and pain. He treats us with gentle dignity as we weep our tears of sorrow and thankfulness. Here's part of Luke's account of the story.

> 'A sinful woman in the town learned that Jesus was eating at the Pharisee's house. So she brought an alabaster jar of perfume and stood behind Jesus at his feet, crying. She began to wash his feet with her tears, and she dried them with her hair, kissing them many times and rubbing them with the perfume.'
>
> Luke 7:37–38, NCV

As well as her sex we know two things about her: she's a sinner and she's a crier. Tears and trouble often go hand in hand – as do tears and healing. But the Gospel accounts aren't only a story about a woman. They're the story of two men. One, Jesus, who welcomes the tears of a woman, and another, Simon (in some versions it's Judas), who does not. Of course, it's a story ultimately about the nature of God's forgiveness, but it raises some interesting ideas about the significance of our sorrows in how we relate to God.

The art of crying

I for one love a good old cry. Author Paulo Coelho says

that tears are 'words waiting to be written'. I love that. Whenever I'm with someone who is trying to hold back their tears, I encourage them to cry. If what you're feeling is making you cry, then cry. Your tears matter.

A few things have made me bawl my eyes out this week: reading a friend's moving post on Facebook, bashing my head on the corner of a shelf at work and a teenage girl in my youth group telling me that she's beyond ever being loved. All different situations, but all cry-worthy.

Sometimes I feel there's a whole well of tears inside me that need to come out.

Grieving the loss or hurt you feel is essential to finding healing and a way through. Your soul feels pain because your soul is you. Whatever hurts your mind, emotions, heart or body, hurts your soul. Hurts you. Crying, wailing, sobbing, shouting, mourning – all are ways that your body gives flesh and blood expression to the hurt in your soul.

Of course crying isn't the only way we express the hurt we carry. Addictive behaviours, anger, rage, bitterness and despair all betray the sorrows that aren't expressed in grief. Sometimes we find it hard to admit we're hurting. I've worked for years with young women who've been sexually assaulted by men. Because of the situations they were in (either being paid for sex, or being told that sex with one guy would protect them from being raped by the other guys in the gang) many of the women thought they deserved to be hurt like this. A number of them developed addictive behaviours that involved drink, drugs and sex to numb the pain they felt when they were sober or alone. Although to me it seemed so obvious that their souls were wounded, it was incredibly hard for them to see that this was what they were doing. 'If I start thinking about my pain, then how will I get that back in the box so that I can do what I need to do?'

What we need to do, more than anything, is choose life. To do this, we need to grieve the loss and hurt that we carry in the core of our being.

Pain isn't a waste

When I left school after sixth form, I spent a year with a random music group that toured Europe. A good friend was raped and two other friends back at home died in a car crash. It was a bad year and I was angry. With God; with horrible human beings who destroyed other people. Angry at the waste. I began to feel the grief of the home-lessness I'd experienced with my family and the struggle of being the vicar's kid at church and the Christian kid at school. I was losing touch with who I was. The sadness I carried was making me feel broken inside. As if I had shattered into a thousand pieces and was putting myself back together all wrong.

I didn't know what to do. I couldn't find the right words to talk with God about it. When I returned to the UK I took to bashing out my grief on the old piano at my old church, often in pitch darkness because I felt freer that way. My soul was crying and the keys on the piano pulled the wail out of me. Slowly, very slowly, I began to notice that God was prepared to be with me in the dark corners of my grief, when I didn't really know what I was feeling, and when all I wanted to do was link a load of swear words together and hurl them at him.

'Why didn't you stop these things happening?'

'Why do you hurt the people you say you love?'

'Why do you stand by and let me hurt?'

I found no answers to my big questions. I still have many of the same questions! But as I let it all come to the surface, unchecked, I felt a heavy weight lift from my soul and life began to flow through me again. My soul began to heal as I leaned on God who was reaching out to me, beyond simple answers and reason, and who was showing me that my pain is never a waste.

'Why are you in despair, my soul? Why are you disturbed within me? Hope in God, because I will praise him once again, since his presence saves me and he is my God.'

Psalm 43:5, ISV

We experience sorrow because we're experiencing life. None of us can avoid being hurt, but what we can do is allow the hurt we feel to draw us closer to God. Nothing in my life makes me more dependent on God than when I'm struggling to cope. I pray more and seek God more when I feel at the end of what I can achieve. This is how God transforms us *through* our sufferings, so by inviting him to help us respond to our hurts with even greater trust in what he can do, we're opening ourselves up to the good that he can bring about in any and each situation.

'As my sufferings mounted, I soon realized that there were two ways that I could respond to my situation: either to react with bitterness or seek to transform the suffering into a creative force. I decided to follow the latter course.'

Martin Luther King Jr, *Suffering and Faith*[2]

Soulful

Finding God's goodness at the place of pain is something that Hagar experienced too. She was the only person in the Bible to ever give a name to God. This abused single mother, an immigrant sex slave, pregnant with her master Abraham's baby, was alone in a wilderness (Genesis 16). We can only assume that she faced the risk of wild animals and a lack of water, food and shelter was because death was better than staying put in a place where she was being treated so badly.

But it's here, at her moment of greatest despair, that she experiences the loving gaze of God. He asks her what she's doing. 'Running away from Sarah, who's abusing me,' comes Hagar's reply. God tells her to go home, which I find so uncomfortable. How can he ask her to go back to the people who are hurting her? Why doesn't he rescue her? There are no easy answers.

But something happens out in the wilderness that transforms Hagar. She is seen by God. Look at what she says: 'She gave this name to the LORD who spoke to her: "You are the God who sees me," for she said, "I have now seen the One who sees me"' (Genesis 16:13, NIV). She could of course simply be referring to God noticing the physical state of her situation. But have you ever come back from a meeting with your course tutor or line manager and felt utterly transformed by the fact that they've noticed you're under a lot of pressure? No! It's nice to have that stuff acknowledged, but it's not ultimately life-changing. What *is* life-changing is seeing with your soul the one who sees you in your soul. This is deep crying out to deep (Psalm 42:7). *This* is what heals our souls. When you're hurting, the only thing that soothes the soul is the powerful presence of the one who has been through suffering and death, and has come out the other side with the keys to life in his hands!

Why does life hurt?

There are hurts that are inflicted on us, wilfully. Where someone has made it their business to hurt us. Whether it's physical, emotional, sexual or spiritual, it's deliberate and often persistent. It's hardest when it comes from people close to us, who get to us when our guard is down.

Then there are hurts we carry that are due to the things that come our way. Someone's senseless actions may be the cause of pain in our lives but it's more random than deliberate. I find this often the hardest to understand. How is it possible to just be in the wrong place at the wrong time and die in a car crash?

But sometimes we experience suffering because we're living in a world with decay and disease. Being a follower of Jesus doesn't act as a guarantee against sickness and accidents. My own infertility falls into this one.

In my twenties and early thirties, never being able to

have my own children felt like an overwhelming sadness. Conceiving a baby seemed like the most natural and significant indicator of my female identity. I didn't live to have kids; I enjoyed an exciting career and loved the freedom of doing my own thing whenever I wanted. But the failure and crippling sadness I felt as we realised we wouldn't have our own children drove me deep into a shame I'd never known before. I knew rationally that it wasn't my 'fault' but that didn't bring me any comfort. Seeing my friends with their babies hurt. Seeing pregnant women on the street hurt. Navigating the world of pregnancy announcements on social media, shower parties and the inevitable 'Rachel, do you *want* children?' line of questioning hurt. Loving and prayerful people gave my husband and me significant words from God about how many children I would give birth to, including their sex. It was well meaning, but still hurtful.

I went searching for someone who knew what I was going through – my 'hurt-ally'. I found her in the pages of a book of the Bible called Samuel. Ironic, seeing as it was the name of the son she eventually gave birth to. But when I read her prayer of anguish I knew I had found a soul-sister. Because the thing about hurt is that it can become toxic. Like a wound that's left undressed can become infected, so too with our emotional and spiritual wounds. More than anything I didn't want to become a hard shell of a person. If hurting was my way of knowing I was still alive and open to love, then I would prefer to hurt than to feel nothing.

So Hannah dropped into my life. Separated by thousands of years and eons of culture, I consumed her story. I soon discovered that what looked like a story about the pain of infertility was also about the pain of female friendship and the damage to women of the practice of polygamy. The focus of the story is on these women, Peninah and Hannah, who are forced together in marriage to the same man, Elkanah. At Hannah's moment of vulnerability, she is wounded by his other wife, Peninah, who knows Hannah's pain in being childless yet chooses to become her enemy instead of her friend. *The Message* explains it like this: 'But her rival wife taunted her cruelly, rubbing it in and never letting her forget that GOD had not given her children' (1 Samuel 1:6).

But then we read that after a year of hanging back and quietly nursing her grief, Hannah does something that changes her relationship with God: she prays. She falls on her knees and pleads with God to hear her. She upsets Eli the Priest, who thinks she's drunk.

'It so happened that as she continued in prayer before GOD, Eli was watching her closely. Hannah was praying in her heart, silently. Her lips moved, but no sound was heard. Eli jumped to the conclusion that she was drunk. He approached her and said, "You're drunk! How long do you plan to keep this up? Sober up, woman!" Hannah said, "Oh no, sir—please! I'm a woman hard used. I haven't been drinking. Not a drop of wine or beer. The only thing I've been pouring out is my heart, pouring it out to GOD. Don't for a minute think I'm a bad woman. It's because I'm so desperately unhappy and in such pain that I've stayed here so long."'

1 Samuel 1:12–16, *The Message*

Have you had a close friend set themselves against you? Or people you've trusted take delight in tearing you down? It *hurts*. First there's shock, then questions. What did I do wrong? How long have they been planning this? What have I missed? The shock that comes with the hurt we feel means we're not sure who we can trust. So instead of reaching out we shut down, licking our wounds. The problem with nursing your own wounds is that you don't let God close.

My daughter once fell off a swing and cut her knee badly. Blood was everywhere. Pretty impressive fall. But she didn't want me to look. She hunched her little body around her knee and kept brushing my hand away. I was heartbroken hearing her little sobs. But I didn't leave her. She's mine. 'I'm here, darling. Let me look. I've got this,' I kept murmuring over and over again. Eventually she let me in, and I cleaned it up (more screaming!), popped a plaster on and she was off again.

But that's because she was three years old and she had just cut her knee. Those hurts heal pretty quickly. But what of the hurts that take years to heal? The wounds that are so deep, they're almost impossible to see? How do those heal?

What hurts do you carry?

Sometimes I notice a tendency in women to rate their pain, as if some things are worthy of our attention and others are not. I remember once saying to a kind friend who was empathising with me about my infertility, 'Yes, but I've never conceived and had a miscarriage like you have. How do I have the right to tell you about my struggles? What you've been through is so much worse.' She told me off, right there and then!

'Rachel, your pain is no less painful because it's not like mine. If your soul is hurting it's hurting! Don't compare it.'

She's right. If your soul is hurt, it matters that you listen to yourself.

Say your name

In his brilliant book *Soulfulness*[3] my friend Brian Draper suggests a gentle practice to help you listen to your soul. I have discovered it helps me to find where my soul is hurting. He suggests that you find space in your day where you won't be interrupted. Take a few moments to settle yourself; find a comfortable seat, switch off your phone and remove anything that would distract you by beeping or flashing at you!

Then say your name.

Just say it. Gently. *Rachel*. Then say it again. And again. Leave a gap of a few seconds between each time you say it.

Whenever I feel out of kilter with myself, I do this. I know that as I speak my name, God calls my name too. It's as if I'm being woken up to a deeper sense of myself. I use this as a powerful way in to speaking with God about the hurt I'm carrying inside. So as well as speaking out *your* name before God, find a word or two that names the hurt you feel. It doesn't have to make sense to anyone else. As you sit in silence, begin to speak out these words to God. I do this as a way to acknowledge before God that he has my permission to take this hurt and use it in any way he sees fit to bring about my healing and also enable me to serve others better.

The Psalms were written from the depths of raw human emotion and pain. This particular psalm was written by David when he was a prisoner of war in Philistine.

> 'You keep track of all my sorrows.
> You have collected all my tears in your bottle.
> You have recorded each one in your book.'
>
> Psalm 56:8, NLT

In ancient times, mourners would capture their tears in a jar to be buried with their deceased loved one. In writing this, David expresses his deep grief but also deep trust that God not only hears his pain but remembers it. God doesn't keep a track of our sins but he keeps a track of our pain. That's awe-inspiring, isn't it? Not a single one of your tears falls without God knowing and remembering.

From the depths of his soul, David's words reach out to a time when no more tears will need to be collected and remembered; when God will make all things new. His plan was never for us to suffer and die. In these words, written by John, you can hear the fury against pain and death in God's voice as he brings an end to the old order and ushers in a new heaven and a new earth:

> 'I heard a voice thunder from the Throne: "Look! Look! God has moved into the neighborhood, making his home with men and women! They're his people, he's their God. He'll wipe every tear from their eyes. Death is gone for good—tears gone, crying gone, pain gone—all the first

order of things gone." The Enthroned continued, "Look! I'm making everything new."'

Revelation 21:4–5, *The Message*

Say your name. Name your pain.

The art of lamenting

But although there will come a time when we won't be crying and hurting any more, I'm not going to give up on crying anytime soon. I think there are things in our own lives and in others that we *only* see when we cry. Victor Hugo in *Les Miserables* remarks, 'Those who do not weep, do not see.' Which makes me wonder if maybe there are things we can only see when we mourn. Are there ways of connecting deeply with each other that can only happen when we have tears running down our faces? Are there opportunities for growth in your calling and ministry that are made more possible by a good old cry for and with the people you serve?

We can begin by naming what's broken in us: our vanity, fear, greed, insecurity, faithlessness. This is because some of the hurts we suffer come from our own dis-ease with ourselves, our world, each other and God. It hurts me that I am impatient and easily angry with the people closest to me. When I see the look of hurt on my mum's face after I've exploded at her out of my own frustration, it hurts. I need to lament my brokenness, and ask God to heal me so that I don't pass my hurt on to others.

It's important that when you're hurt you grieve. Otherwise you're anchoring your soul to a hurt that remains raw and will continue to hurt. Give yourself the time to feel what you're feeling, without judgement or analysis. Friends who are good at being with you without needing to 'talk it out' are a real blessing at this point. You might need to sit quietly for a long time. They need to be OK with that. But you will at some point need to talk it out because we need to face and mourn what is broken and desolate in us and around us. If we don't mourn we don't mend.

But it doesn't stop here. The moment we look beyond ourselves we can see what's broken in our homes, communities, local authorities, churches, businesses, universities and workplaces. At some point the tears might bubble up to the surface. Don't hold back – let them flow. Let the ache you feel about what you see lead you into lament and into a deeper connection with others who suffer.

> '. . . the ideas in our minds are not enough to change the world, because it's really what's in your heart that gets you to do the things that seem a little dangerous, that seem a little edgy, that push you into these spaces that are uncomfortable. Ideas are meaningless unless fueled by some conviction in our hearts.'
>
> Bryan Stevenson[4]

Lament is a passionate, raw expression of sorrow. It's an ancient art that we've mostly lost touch with. A lot of the Psalms are laments to God against the injustice of suffering in the world. The writers are getting brutally honest with God, demanding to know where he is and why he's allowed terrible things to happen –

'God, God . . . my God!
Why did you dump me
miles from nowhere?
Doubled up with pain, I call to God
all the day long. No answer. Nothing.
I keep at it all night, tossing and turning.'

Psalm 22:1–2, *The Message*

This doesn't sound like a lot of the prayers we hear in church! I wish we lamented more in our worship services.

But the thing about lament is that it's not crying out *about* God; it's crying out *to* God. It's a deeply trusting thing to do. We shout out our sorrow to the only one who can do anything productive with it!

Because some things are *not* easily fixed. They might never be fixed this side of eternity. The only thing we can do with them is mourn and lament the pain and hurt that is caused. No one teaches us to cry. It's the first thing we do as we burst into the world on day one! But lamenting is different. It's the sound we make as we lean into the reality of living in a broken and suffering world and pour out the pain we're carrying and the hurt we feel.

Don't hide your hurt

The first thing I do when I cry is hide my face behind my hands. It's such a natural thing to do. I'm not sure if it's learned behaviour (probably) or some instinctive way that we seek to protect ourselves at our most vulnerable (probably this too). Many of us hide our emotional pain because we're afraid we'll look weak or be opening ourselves to more pain. We put up walls around us with signs like 'I'm fine, leave me alone' all over them. No one is fooled, but if we do it long enough people will give up trying to get through. And that can hurt even more!

Not many people like confrontation, but allowing people to see when they have hurt us is important. If you've been hurt, you don't need to pretend that it didn't happen. So many of us try to tidy our upsets away in the cupboard under the stairs, but that cupboard door is bulging and the lock won't hold for much longer. It's a standing joke in my family that I'm the person who will make the house look tidy by stuffing everything away in drawers and cupboards! It works, to a point, but there will always come a day when I fling open the cupboard to grab a coat and a whole pile of stuff falls down on me. That's the thing with the hurts we try to shove away from sight. They're waiting for us, and we'll come face to face with them when we least expect it.

But this doesn't need to be the case. You can help people to see the consequences of their actions – even if they didn't mean to hurt you. This is not about getting revenge. If getting your own back is what's motivating you, then this won't work. The only way this is good for your soul is if your desire for life is greater than your desire to pass on the hurt.

Explain to them how their words or actions have hurt you. This is not about blame, so instead of saying something like, 'You totally disrespected me and treated me like rubbish!' it's more effective to say, 'When you shouted at me in front of all those people, I felt completely disrespected by you.' This is also your opportunity to express how the conflict can end by asking for their point of view, and also asking for what you need: 'I need you to speak to me in a calm and respectful way.'

Of course, sometimes we find ourselves facing people who don't care whether they've hurt us or not. This approach still works, because it enables you to say what you need to say, and rise above the game of blame and defence they want to play.

It helps to think about what you want to say beforehand so you don't get drawn into the blame game or forget to say what's on your heart. There have been times when I've asked a friend to come with me or sit in on a phone call, to help me stick to what it is I wanted to say. But as far as you can, be the person to name the hurt your soul carries.

They might apologise to you. But even if they don't, you are choosing life for your soul. The damage of the hurt they have caused can stop here, with you.

The promise of new life

At the start of this chapter I said that our pain is never wasted.

That can sound like an empty promise if you're suffering or in pain. I'm not trying to give you a soundbite to ease the pain or fix your troubles. Jesus doesn't do that, so neither should we. Instead, what we see in Scripture is a promise that we will experience life in the places of our deepest sorrow. We know that God doesn't always change our circumstances. He could! But there are times when he chooses not to. I think this is because he's more interested in changing us. In using the suffering we face to transform us. As we allow him to take and mould us through our hurt, he teaches us to lean on him. To come to him with our hurts and despair, knowing that he will turn our tears into life-giving water and our soul into a wide open space that produces new life.

'When they walk through the Valley of Weeping, it will become a place of refreshing springs. The autumn rains will clothe it with blessings.'

Psalm 84:6, NLT

Jason and I came to adoption after years of failed fertility treatment. It took a while to work through the pain and disappointment of not having birth children. More specifically, of not having our prayers for birth children answered. Then we adopted our small daughter. She arrived in our lives one snowy January. She was ours and a complete stranger at the same time. So we loved and we grew to love, and the hardest times became the means of us becoming a family. After she'd been with us for two years Jason went away on a relief trip to Malawi and I wondered how our daughter would handle the separation. She had bonded so well with me, but was still a little unsure of the big ginger guy who was her dad!

On the day he came home we went to the airport armed with a homemade banner and our daughter dressed in her finest princess outfit. The plane was delayed. By the time it finally landed, this little four-year-old was beside herself with sugary drinks and desperation to go home. In trepidation I led us back to the arrivals lounge, certain that this was going to be a disastrous reunion. We stood opposite the arrivals doors, and my little girl shouted crossly to each passenger who walked through, 'You're not my daddy!'

Eventually Jason appeared, exhausted and in need of a hot shower. I don't think he was ready for what came next. Suddenly his little girl shouted at the top of her voice, 'You're my daddy!' as she ducked under the rails and threw herself at him.

I learned something about hurt and healing that day. We may think we know what we need to soothe our hurts or numb our pain. But in the end, what we need most is to run like a child into the arms of her loving Father who is her refuge and strength. She finds that his hope becomes her hope. His peace, her peace. His wholeness, her wholeness.

This is my story of experiencing the redeeming love of my adoptive heavenly Father who reached out to me when I was lost in my pain and drew me into his heart for good. He never stops.

This is your story too.

'May you have courage to let go of the things that are diminishing you and strength to carry the things that weigh heavy on you.

May you find your brokenness healed and your rough edges challenged.

May you never be afraid of your shadow but may you always be brave enough to lean in to what is dark and unknown in order to find and reveal the light.

May you find souls who will walk with you and alongside you and believe in you as you live your story out loud.

May you never forget that you can make this world a more glorious place to live in, for everyone, simply by loving others as yourself.

And may you always always always know the voice of God calling you by name in all that life is for you.'

Jill Rowe[5]

De-construct me

Everybody hurts. It's an obvious thing to say, but it needs to be said because we live in a society where we're expected not to make a fuss and 'get over it'. But this doesn't work and we discover that few people are prepared to hear it or when they do, we're treated as a failure for being fragile so we eventually learn to cover up our pain and bottle up our feelings. But hurts don't need to be trapped in bottles; they need to be heard.

Here are some questions to help you consider how you listen to the hurt you carry:

- When you're feeling hurt, what do you tend to do?
- Do you give yourself permission to cry, shout or express in your own way the hurt that you feel?
- What's the best way for you to explore why you're feeling hurt? It could be talking it through with someone or spending time alone listening to your soul.
- What stops you speaking with someone about how you feel?
- Do you make inner promises like, 'I'll *never* let myself get hurt again'? Is this something you can actually

promise yourself? What might happen if you didn't make these promises to yourself that you can't keep?

- If someone told you about a sorrow in their life, how would you respond to them? Think about why you don't offer the same loving attention to your own wounded soul as you do to other people.

Re-construct me

But as well as being heard, something needs to happen to the hurts that we feel. Often we think that what will help us the most is to know why something has happened to us. We all want reassurance that the painful things we go through happen for a reason. But even though God works everything out for our good, he doesn't always give us answers to why we're experiencing hurt and pain. Why does God allow my friend to experience a miscarriage or a young person in my youth group to experience bullying at school? I don't know. But I do know that God is always with us, and that no amount of pain or suffering can stop us knowing his love and peace. A book in the Bible that elsewhere makes very little sense to me has this incredibly powerful statement: 'The eternal God is your refuge, And underneath are the everlasting arms' (Deuteronomy 33:27, TLB). This is what I've experienced time and again – I may not have the answers I want, but I have the presence of God that I need.

When we've been hurt, we don't automatically switch into recovery mode – we have to take steps in allowing ourselves time to process what we're feeling. Once you have acknowledged your need for God to heal the hurts that you're experiencing, here are some simple things you can do:

Spend time with God – it can be the hardest thing to accept, but God is always with you, even in the midst of your pain. Sitting alone with God to listen to him, and reading Scripture to hear his voice, creates an openness in you to receive the peace and love of God. I know a woman who writes on tiny pieces of paper 'God is with me' and sticks them inside her shoe or sews them into the hem of her sleeve. She does this because during the day she wants to remind herself that God is always close by, whatever her circumstances.

Forgive those who have hurt you – forgiving someone isn't the same as pretending they didn't hurt you. Forgiving them means you're not going to allow the hurt they've caused to create a hardness and bitterness to grow in your soul. If the pain you're going through is not down to a person but circumstance, you can still choose to let go of the bitterness that wants to take root.

Be sensitive to your healing – if you broke your leg or cut your arm, you wouldn't expect to be up walking again or doing the washing up within moments of being hurt. Even with the cast or bandage on, you would still make sure that you weren't putting too much weight on that part of your body to enable healing to happen uninter-rupted. It's the same with the emotional wounds we carry. As you are choosing to forgive and receive from God, be mindful of how weak you might still be to being hurt again. Although I experienced God healing me of the deep pain of infertility, I knew that I wouldn't be able to run my best friend's baby shower party or be the first to offer to babysit until I felt strong enough to do this with an open heart. This leads us on to the final idea . . .

Serve others – this might sound like the last thing we want to do with the pain we've experienced but as we reach out to others, God transforms our pain from being something that isolates us to something that acts as a bridge between us and others who are suffering too. It's true that unless you've walked a mile in another person's shoes, you can't claim to understand what they're going through. Well, this is the mile you've walked in the same shoes. You may have experienced pain differently, but you will have a deep compassion that is born out of what you have been through.

'And when you draw close to God, God will draw close to you . . .'

James 4:8, TLB

9.

RADIANT

I'm not a huge *Doctor Who* fan, so to be honest when the rumours emerged that the thirteenth incarnation of the Doctor might be a woman, I didn't take much notice. I'm not sure that stories *need* to have female leads to be good news for girls. All the previous Doctors have had mighty female companions who basically make it all happen. They travel the universe with him, kicking cyber butt and delivering their killer lines. Who can ever forget Rose Tyler's outburst at the thought of going back to her ordinary life when she had the chance to travel with the Doctor again?

> 'What do I do every day, Mum? What do I do? I get up, catch the bus, go to work, come back home, eat chips and go to bed!'[1]

So I was totally unprepared for my reaction to the trailer for the new season, where a dark figure walks through the woods to a clearing, pushes back their hood and reveals the face of a *female* Time Lord.

'It's a girl!' screamed kids (and adults) around the globe. We saw them on social media: girls with eyes glued to the screens, their families filming the moment when they caught a glimpse of those hands, that eye, that face! It was an explosion of joy at seeing someone like them being chosen to save the world!

The big reveal is a classic plot device in storytelling. You *think* you know what's coming (yet another white man playing the Doctor) but you don't, as in the blink of an eye everything changes. These are my favourite kinds of plot lines where you don't know how on earth it's all going to end, and just when you think it's all over, the twist comes and you go home happy.

But as predictable as many plot lines are, there's nothing predictable about real life! Good things don't always happen to good people. In the end the guy doesn't always get the girl of his dreams (and vice versa). As we saw in the last chapter, we can be hurt whether we've done the right things or not. Your soul cannot avoid pain, but it can avoid joy.

Joy can be hard to define. It's more than a happiness based on circumstances. It doesn't just happen because there's an alignment in the stars or a new incarnation of the Time Lord. Joy isn't a plot line in someone else's story because somehow they're more deserving of happiness. Joy is something we invite into our lives.

Research professor Brené Brown shot to fame in June 2010 when she gave a TED talk on the power of vulnerability.[2] Eleven thousand conversations with people about how they experienced courage, vulnerability, empathy and shame had thrown up some contradictions that Brené wanted to share. Among other revelations, Brené discovered something incredible about the way we find joy. 'I didn't meet anyone who would describe themselves as a joyful person who didn't actively practice gratitude.' For

Brené what she was hearing was more than people's 'attitude of gratitude'; she was seeing how *practising* gratitude invites joy into lives. She quotes a Jesuit priest who once said, 'It's not joy that makes us grateful; it's gratitude that makes us joyful.'

We invite joy into our soul not by *feeling* grateful, but by *doing* grateful.

Gratitude gives us a soulful window into what we're able to recognise as good in our lives. You might *say* you're grateful for your noisy neighbours keeping you up all night as it made you finish your assignment, but you don't really mean it! Gratitude connects our souls to what we believe gives our lives true meaning and purpose. It is an acknowledgement of the preciousness of what we've already received. As we recognise that we are receiving what we don't deserve, deep thankfulness is formed in us, opening us up to the gift of joy.

The Bible reveals a similar path to inviting joy into our lives. We can't make ourselves *feel* joy, because we're not the source of it. But as God is the source of it, we can *receive* it.

Joy is poured into our souls because of the grace of God in our lives. It's not because of our circumstances or whether we've done anything to deserve it. In Scripture, joy is the fruit of the gratitude that comes when we recognise and trust everything Christ *is* and everything he has given us. 'You love him', observes Jesus' close friend, 'even though you have never seen him; though not seeing him, you trust him; and even now you are happy with the inexpressible joy that comes from heaven itself' (1 Peter 1:8–9, TLB).

This ability to behold Jesus in all his beauty and majesty is the work of the Holy Spirit in our lives. This is what Peter means by us not being able to see him in bodily form any more. The Spirit reveals Jesus to us: his beauty, his power, his glory. It's as if the Spirit pulls back the curtains in our soul and says to us, 'Look! Look at how breathtaking Jesus is! Fix your eyes on him. Don't stop gazing at his beauty. See how even the brightest colours and most dazzling lights dim in the brilliance of his brightness.' This is why we invite the Holy Spirit to fill us as we worship Jesus. Because in helping us to recognise Jesus, he draws gratitude up from the depth of our souls and joy pours out from heaven to meet it!

What a glorious showdown!

When did you last linger in the presence of God, longing to do nothing more than gaze on Jesus' beauty and majesty? As we gaze on Jesus our problems don't disappear, but we gain a new perspective on them. As Jesus begins to fill our vision, the circumstances we feel stuck in have to take a back seat. It's not that our problems don't matter, but they don't dictate who we are. We can appreciate all we already have and are because of Christ. We are loved, forgiven, chosen, free, called and equipped by God. As we turn our attention to gratitude, joy has room to grow in us – the joy that comes from dependence on God, his power and goodness. This is why we can be joyful in the toughest of times. Our circumstances might be great or terrible. We might have everything going for us or everything against us. But we are joyful, because we are grateful for Jesus. Our life flows from the unspeakable debt of gratitude we now owe for all we have been given in him.

Who would you say has a radiant, joy-filled life?

I don't mean who do you know who's nice or bubbly! They might be these things as well, but joy is so much deeper. It's most often found in the lives of people who've carried a lot of pain and hurt but have chosen life for their soul. By doing so, they've invited joy into their lives. I know someone who has been through hell. You name it, she's faced it. She's a passionate advocate for other women who suffer. Her informed opinions and prophetic insight mean you wouldn't want to mess with her! But if you were to be in her presence, even for a moment, you would experience joy radiating out of her. She's chosen to direct the flow of her life in loving gratitude for all Jesus has freed her from and for. Her courage and joy are contagious.

That's the thing about joy. It shines.

Shiny grace

In Old Testament times, slaves had to cover their faces before their masters. Even God's chosen prophets, priests and kings couldn't have free access to God's presence (the Holy of Holies) in the Jewish Temple. The thought of looking on the face of God would have filled the ancients with fear and trembling. God is utterly holy and we are not; no one gets to see Almighty God and live (Exodus 33:19–23).

But all that changes in Jesus. He is holy fire with skin on! He is fully God and fully human. Because Jesus has gone through death and been raised to life again, we don't need to cover our faces from God for fear of being destroyed. When we accept the sacrifice that Jesus made of himself on our behalf we are free to gaze on the glory of God, mirrored in Jesus, who is the visible image of the invisible God (Colossians 1:15). The light reflected from God *in* Jesus shines on us, lighting us up, like a beam of sunlight reflected through a mirror. This is how we physically radiate the glory of Jesus – and people can see it!

When I met Emilia it was like looking into a fire. She crackled with so much energy and passion for God, it lit her up from the inside. She'd only recently become a Christian after years of feeling so lost in her own sense of failure. 'I'm alive now!' she said. 'I was dying inside and so lost. I couldn't sit my exams and felt my life crumbling around my ears.' Then she allowed herself to be dragged to a Christian festival where she heard and saw evidence of God's existence and love for her. She showed me a drawing she'd made of a woman, lying on her back, with a huge dazzling cloud of bright colours hovering above her that was pouring itself into this woman's navel.

'This is what it feels like to me to know God. All his life is being poured into me. I can't contain the joy I feel!' she said.

'I can see all this,' I said, pointing to the colours and brightness. 'I can see all this pouring *out* of you.'

The joy Emilia was experiencing at receiving God's grace and forgiveness was making her face shine! I almost can't remember the specific features of her face, but I'll never forget the look of joy glowing from her soul. She was radiant, she was beautiful.

This is the potential for soulful beauty that lies within each one of us. It's not what is prescribed and defined by a toxic beauty industry culture where women are judged on how they look. I'm talking about the look on our faces as we receive God's grace and forgiveness. Being free makes you beautiful!

I love the chance to dress up and express my uniqueness through fashion, make-up and completely impractical shoes. But nothing takes my breath away like the brilliance of a woman giving flesh and blood expression to the real gratitude she feels deep within her soul. This is the beauty that we're made to be. It's not conditioned by culture or mass produced in media. Glamour (clothes, hairstyles, fashion, make-up, perfume) comes and goes. Beauty lingers. It is the joy that lingers in a room long after we've left. It's the possibility for hope that people catch when they look into our eyes. It is the glow of a face that's been gazing at Jesus.

'Look to him and be radiant.'

Psalm 34:5, ISV

Practices of gratitude

How do we 'do' grateful?

The best way to start is small. Look out for the small moments during the day when someone does something unexpected for you that you appreciate. Or did you catch sight of something when you were out and about that made you smile? If it feels too small to be thankful for, then it's exactly what you *should* be thankful for!

There was a book on the shelf at home when I was a kid that traced the journey of a glass of water all the way back past the people who made the taps, pipes and water purification units, to the God who created the world in the first place. The idea was that a tiny 'thank you' whispered to an inanimate object will inevitably lead to a mighty 'thank you' bellowed out to the expanse of sky!

GRATITUDE MAKES US PAY ATTENTION TO THE SWEETNESS OF GOD'S PRESENCE IN OUR LIVES.
Imagine using that principle with every tiny moment of gratitude. As you walk past a park, you see a shaft of light falling onto a bench where a woman is sitting. You don't tweet or Instagram it. This is not a moment for the world. It's a moment for your soul. You notice it and imagine sitting in the warmth of God's light. You're grateful that wherever you are, God's love will find you. You walk on with more of a lightness in your step. And the next person you connect with senses something deeper in you.

But when you get home, your mum tells you there won't be much for dinner. In fact there's only a couple of potatoes, and no money to buy any more food until the benefits come at the end of the week. It's a bleak dinner in an unheated house. But your dad, who must be struggling with the situation, still says 'grace' before the meagre meal, and means every word. 'We are grateful to you, Lord, for all we have.' Then there's a knock on the door. A stranger stands in the doorway with a platter of left-over party food. 'I really hope you don't mind me turning up like this. We've got all this food left over and didn't want it to go to waste. Would you like it?'

God could have asked her to write a cheque for £100

– that would have really helped my family that night! But my parents received the leftovers with so much gratitude overflowing from their hearts. To them this was another example of the gracious provision of a Father who never abandons us. I have never heard my parents do anything but express genuine gratitude to God for all he has given them. They are two of the most beautiful people I will ever know. I am eternally grateful for their example.

GRATITUDE MAKES US PAY ATTENTION TO THE DIGNITY AND HUMANITY IN OTHER PEOPLE'S LIVES. As well as recognising the moments each day where we can be grateful, expressing our gratitude to others changes our relationships with them. I make a point of thanking everyone who serves or helps me. It doesn't put me in their debt. Simply saying 'thank you' rather than 'thanks' has a significant effect! Every time we acknowledge someone for what they have done for us, we are recognising the image of God in them. We are connecting with them from our soul.

GRATITUDE MAKES IT POSSIBLE FOR US TO SLOW DOWN AND TAKE IN MORE OF THE WONDER AROUND US.
Taking the time to notice all the things in our lives we can be thankful for has the knock-on effect of slowing us down a bit. We can't stop to smell the coffee if we don't stop! I still live at a pretty hectic pace most of the time – but practising gratitude, has drawn into my life the chance to pause and let the light in. I've found I need to get practical about gratitude, so I have a poster on the

wall encouraging me to get outside, and post-it notes all over the place encouraging me to name what I'm grateful for. Stock up on some postcards or make your own cards online so that you don't have an excuse not to send thank you notes to people who have blessed you.

GRATITUDE RELEASES US TO LOOK BEYOND OURSELVES.

But there's one final element to gratitude that I want to share. We don't often experience ourselves as the precious women we are. We're painfully aware of our flaws and selfishness. This can be such a barrier to living soulful lives. We believe that if we don't like what's at our core, no one else will either. But this is where growing in gratitude and joyfulness comes in. We don't 'do' grateful to like ourselves more, but as we grow in gratitude we like ourselves more! We get to experience ourselves as generous, giving, radiant people. Paying attention to the treasures that come our way every day, and opening up our souls to receive them, means we are less self-absorbed.

Don't be a killjoy

If it's possible to invite joy into our lives, it's also possible to kill joy.

Meet John Gottman, Professor Emeritus of Psychology at the University of Washington, who claims that within moments of meeting a married couple he can predict, with a high degree of accuracy, whether they will get divorced in the next few years or not. Fun guy to have at a dinner party! This certainty comes from over forty years of research in his 'Love Lab' (yes, that's a real thing) where his team videotaped thousands of newlywed couples discussing a combative topic for fifteen minutes to measure precisely *how* they fought over it. The exchange would be coded and the team then predicted which marriages would survive the next few years and which would end in divorce. Sure enough, three to six years later when the team checked in with the same couples, their predictions were right – to 94 per cent accuracy![3]

How did they do it? How could they possibly know how a marriage would fare? They couldn't predict the future or guess the stresses and strains each couple might be under. Surely, the more difficulty a couple faced, the greater likelihood that they would split up?

No.

It had nothing to do with what the couples faced; it was all to do with *how* the couples faced it. In the short interviews the experts were looking for something very specific that they nick-named the 'Four Horsemen': defensiveness, stonewalling, criticism and contempt. But, says Gottman, the most toxic of these is contempt.

Contempt says that *I* matter and *you* don't.

It's the belief that as the other person is worth less than me, they don't deserve my gratitude or generosity. So my attitude towards them is disapproval mixed with disgust. 'Having someone you love express contempt toward you is so stressful that it begins to affect the functioning of your immune system,' says Gottman.

Acts of contempt are invariably directed towards people we feel are lower than us. They can seem pretty innocuous: rolling your eyes at someone you think is an idiot, cutting into traffic at the junction because it's beneath you to queue up with everyone else, or sucking your teeth at the cashier who dropped your change by mistake as he handed it to you. We're all capable of acting with disdain towards others. But how can we lord it over other people, when the one person who could legitimately lord it over us comes to us as a humble servant? Our contempt of others deeply dishonours Jesus. So we need to check our contempt before it corrodes our generosity, undermining our practices of gratitude.

How do we check our contempt? We ask the Spirit to help us recognise the lordship of Jesus and our need for him, that without him we have nothing. Then we begin to speak out our gratitude for all we have been given in Jesus that we don't deserve.

As we practise gratitude by fixing our eyes on Jesus and receiving the joy God pours into our lives, we begin to experience the life we were always meant to live. And somehow, incredibly, what shines out of us is a radiance that lingers. It might take us by surprise, that we could shine like this. But why not? We belong to the God whose glory fills the heavens. When we're looking at him, how could we do anything but shine?

'We are all meant to shine, as children do. We were born to make manifest the glory of God that is within us. It is not just in some of us; it is in everyone and as we let our own light shine, we unconsciously give others permission to do the same.'

Marianne Williamson, *A Return to Love*[4]

Shine on.

De-construct me

What stops you from practising gratitude in your everyday life? Be as specific as you can. Once you've identified what's holding you back, think about how you'd like your gratitude to look. Do you want more confidence to thank people, or more time to notice the good things you already have in your life? These goals are good! They are also doable, by you! Confidence is the result of experience, so if you want more confidence to say thank you, then say thank you. To begin with you may feel uncomfortable. But you'll realise it wasn't that bad, and actually that person really appreciated you saying it. So that grows your confidence to take more risks in practising gratitude. The same applies to wanting more time. Even if you don't believe it, you're in charge of your time. We tend to make time for the things that matter to us. So even if it's just ten seconds here or a passing moment there, manage your time so that you can become a woman who recognises the sweet presence of God at work in and all around you.

Re-construct me

You're created to know deep joy, even in the middle of challenges and struggles. For Paul, everything is an opportunity to declare his joy in knowing Jesus. Joy is like an arrow, deep within his soul, pointing to Jesus. I call the presence of joy in my life my 'Yeah, but . . .'. We don't for a moment pretend things aren't tough when they are. Paul doesn't pull any punches – he tells us all the rubbish he's had to contend with. But in his soul his 'Yeah, but . . .' points him to the grace he has received because of Jesus. This is the unquenchable source of his joy.

Read his brilliant rant against the idea that a tough life would stop him radiating joy. In fact for Paul, his struggles lead him to gratitude for all he has in Jesus. (I've added in the 'yeah, but . . .' bits!)

'People are watching us as we stay at our post, alertly, unswervingly . . . in hard times, tough times, bad times; when we're beaten up, jailed, and mobbed; working hard, working late; yeah, but . . . with pure heart, clear head, steady hand; in gentleness, holiness, and honest love; when we're telling the truth, and when God's showing his power; when we're doing our best setting things right; when we're praised, and when we're blamed; slandered, and honored; true to our word, though distrusted; ignored by the world, yeah, but . . . recognized by God; terrifically alive, though rumoured to be dead; beaten within an inch of our lives, yeah, but . . . refusing to die; immersed in tears, yeah, but . . . always filled with deep joy; living on handouts, yeah, but . . . enriching many; having nothing, yeah, but . . . having it all.'

2 Corinthians 6:4–12, *The Message*

Imagine writing your own 'yeah, but . . .' passage that might be read by followers of Jesus in years to come. What would you point to as the moments when you experienced the wonder of God's grace, even though the circumstances of your life were difficult? Write some down.

My 'yeah, but . . .' moments:

I have been through . . .

I didn't know if I would be able to cope with . . .

I know that in the future I might experience . . .

Yeah, but . . . I'm still receiving God's love and grace, which means that regardless of my circumstances I can know deep and lasting joy. Whether a smile is on my lips or tears are falling down my face, I radiate the joy of knowing that everything is mine in him.

STRENGTH.

'I raise up my voice – not so I can shout, but so that those without a voice can be heard. We cannot succeed when half of us are held back.'

Malala Yousafzai

'She is clothed with strength and dignity,
and she laughs without fear of the future.'

Proverbs 31:25, NLT

10

POWER

I was raised on girl power.

The moment Geri Halliwell slipped on that infamous Union Jack dress in the late 1990s I knew that life as a member of the female sex would never be the same again. The Spice Girls burst into our lives, pouting and high kicking their singles to number one and their brand of girl power into girls' (and some boys') bedrooms around the globe. This was the era of the teen queen. *Move over, mister, the sisters are doing it for themselves!* As female role models they weren't without their faults; I still can't reconcile their claim to female empowerment with their dressing up as porn stars in bondage gear in one of their music videos. But at a time when I was looking around for role models, these girls who seemed to have talent and power in abundance had me hooked.

I once asked a group of Christian feminist theologians what they thought the church had to say to the Spice Girls. 'Put more clothes on,' smirked one of the women. I couldn't believe it – was that all we had to say? Is it any wonder that the Spice Girls generation, and subsequent generations of women, aren't sure what the Christian faith has to say about female empowerment in the twenty-first century?

In this chapter I'm keen to explore the link between being a woman and power. How do we as Christian women understand and exercise our power? Is it OK to be powerful? Where does our power come from?

Power is a complicated topic for women.

As I write, the female voice has never been so loud, and it's both heartbreaking and inspiring. The global outpouring of women publicly sharing on social media their #metoo stories of assault and abuse by men has shocked society to its core. The fact that women of all colours, backgrounds, faiths and economic and educational status have been subjected to sexualised harm is a reminder that no woman is exempt from the dangers of men who seek to control and demean women. The need for women to insist on their voice being heard and their body being respected is still as great as ever.

Years after the sexual revolution of the sixties, which included giving women control over their fertility and thus being less controlled by men, the new sexual revolution brought about by internet technology seems to be *adding* to female powerlessness through the commodification of women's bodies and lives. The twenty-first-century feminine ideal that rules over culture is exaggerated and unattainable; she supposedly enjoys degradation (thanks, online porn), is flawlessly beautiful (thanks, Instagram) with a perfect partner, kids, job, home and holiday (thanks, Facebook). As women we *are* oppressed by this fake 'perfection'. The options are either to cave in to the deeply entrenched gender norms, be that of the porn sex doll or the long-suffering wife, or to resist and face the shaming and trolling reserved for women who dare to think and act differently. And either way, girls and women risk violence and abuse simply because they're female.

At the same time as this narrowing of the sexualised feminine ideal there are questions being asked in culture right now about what it means to be a woman. 'Is the vagina female?' 'How about attributes like nurture?' 'What's more feminine: a commanding woman or a passive man?' There are challenges to the belief that biology (the bodies we're born with) tells the truth about our gender identity. What happens if you're born male but experience yourself as female? We're also inevitably experiencing a hardening of gender stereotypes in some corners of the Christian community. Many Christian women feel less sure that they're affirmed in their God-given abilities and callings by their church, Christian family or university Christian Union. Men generally still hold the power in the Christian community and define the rules. Women are still missing from many of the platforms and decisions. Women of colour even more so. Not only are non-white women missing from positions of leadership and influence on grounds of their gender, but also on grounds of their race.

I believe this grieves God's heart.

Being female brings with it a set of cultural assumptions that are not attributed to guys. Confident girls are often called 'bossy', whereas confident boys are more likely to be called 'leaders'. Girls should be sexy, but not interested in sex. Boys should be sexually active, but never admit they have feelings. These are poisonous lies that need to be confronted, because no one flourishes in a world like this.

Especially if you're female and poor.

To celebrate the twentieth anniversary of the Spice Girls single 'Wannabe' on 7 July 2017, the Global Goals Campaign released a new music video to go with it, featuring women from around the world, to bring attention to equal rights for girls and women. Watching the new version I felt the single had finally come home. 'Tell me what you want, what you really really want!' takes on a new meaning when you know that around 120 million girls worldwide have been forced to have sex at some point in their lives, and at least 200 million women and girls alive today have been subjected to female genital mutilation in the countries collecting the data. In most of these countries, the majority of girls are cut before the age of five. Women and girls together account for 71 per cent of all those who have been subjected to human trafficking, with girls representing nearly three out of every four children who have been trafficked. Nearly three out of every four trafficked women and girls are trafficked for the purpose of being sexually exploited by men. (All these figures come from reports by the UN.[1])

This is horrifying!

Now tell me what you want, what you really *really* want.

What I want is for men's violence towards women and girls to stop. I want women to have free access to equal opportunities and equal pay to men. I want girls to have access to education, health care and good job opportunities and to grow up without the fear of kidnappers, rapists and slave traders. I want girls in my community to grow up without the fear of men harassing or assaulting them just for walking down the street. I have no doubt that God wants this too.

But it goes further. I know that God has a vision for life

in all its fullness for all of humanity – which includes girls and women. We're called to the adventure of knowing God and pursuing the call he has placed on our lives. So Christian female empowerment is about seeing *all* women fully participating in the life God has given them. Evidence tells us that where women are empowered the economy is more stable, communities are healthier and families are stronger. What a powerful blessing for everyone that comes when women are released to be all God created them to be!

Giving women equal opportunities to men isn't a rebellion against God's created order. And this isn't a world where women lead at the expense of men. We have equality because men and women are made in the same image, God's image: 'He created them male and female' (Genesis 5:2, NIV), and because our redemption is through Jesus 'there is no male and female, for you are all one in Christ Jesus' (Galatians 3:28, ESV). Women being subjected to men is part of the curse of Adam and Eve's disobedience, not how it was ever meant to be.

I know some women struggle with the stories of women in the Bible because they're set in a world where women are victims of their historical context. Some appalling stuff happens to women in Scripture at the hands of godly men that goes unchallenged. Which is why the way Jesus treats women leaps off the page. It was revolutionary then, and it is still revolutionary now. Jesus wasn't just nice to women, he ennobled them!

'Perhaps it is no wonder that the women were the first at the cradle and last at the cross. They had never known a man like this man – there has never been such another.

A prophet and teacher who never nagged at them, never flattered or coaxed or patronised, who never made arch jokes about them . . . who rebuked without [demeaning]; who praised without condescension; who took their questions and arguments seriously; who never mapped out their sphere for them, never urged them to be feminine or jeered at them for being female; who had no axe to grind and no uneasy male dignity to defend . . .'

Dorothy L. Sayers, *Are Women Human?*[2]

There are individual Christians as well as church denominations who point to the inferior role women played in Scripture to reinforce their view that women must be subordinate to men. Esther is a class example. She is sometimes offered as an example of how a Christian wife should be. But she's forced into marriage with a volatile and aggressive man, made to endure the misogyny of his closest advisors and threatened with death if she speaks without permission. Her courage in *not* giving in to this bully saved a nation – and the Bible puts her centre stage.

This is because women in every age and even nation are called and used by God in powerful ways, not because they are women, but because they are *available* to him. In the book of Exodus, enslaved refugee midwives brought illegal baby boys into the world and saved them from death (Exodus 1:17). Deborah steps into a role more usually filled by a man, to show them how it's done (Judges 4:4–10). Abigail bravely changes the course of a king (1 Samuel 25:18–34), and Esther changes the destiny of a nation (Esther 8:5–9). Tamar risks everything to pursue justice (Genesis 38). In the Gospels, Mary demonstrates remarkable obedience to the daunting prospect of being the mother of God (Luke 1:38) and Lydia risks persecution to help plant new churches (Acts 16:14, 40).

Then there's Eve. The first woman in Scripture.

She's created out of Adam's side and called his 'help meet'. I grew up knowing that helping men was a good thing because the guys were the ones with the great ideas and strategic plans, and I had to find a way to encourage them and muck in! I know a lot of wonderful men whom I love cheering on and lending my strength to as we serve God's mission together, but I no longer think I have nothing of my own to bring. This is largely due to a deeper understanding of the meaning of 'help meet'.

It is made up of two Hebrew words: *ezer* and *k'enegdo*. When you do a quick search for where *ezer* appears in the Old Testament you discover that out of the twenty-one times it's used, sixteen times it refers to God as Israel's help in battle! God defines the woman as warrior-hearted and battle-ready! She's Adam's 'help meet' – his suitable and equal partner and she stands up on her own two feet. She's strong-boned, glowing with life and full of dreams and plans for life with Adam in Eden. She is soul, she is body, she is female. Before they fall into sin, Adam and Eve experience mutuality. It's only after the Fall that the power-struggle frames their relationship, and it has devastatingly framed relationships between the sexes ever since.

Beverly Campbell asks us to imagine how different things would be if we had been taught to understand the creation of humans in Eden like this: 'It is not good that man should be alone. I will make him a companion of strength and power who has a saving power and is equal with him.'[3]

If men and women are equal before God then we need the power to make that work in the reality of our lives. We can do this by seeing ourselves as belonging in the spaces of leadership and influence we often feel excluded from. We can do this by encouraging other women, not tearing them down when they faithfully serve God's calling on their life. We can do this by speaking well to and of the men we serve and lead with. We can do this by asking questions about why women are silenced or excluded from certain spaces or decisions. When women are prevented from fully participating in the life of the church, the whole church misses out.

As so many of us have grown up not seeing women represented in the leadership of our churches or denominations, I was keen to see what impact this might have on how Christian teenage girls and young women from across the UK feel about their female identity. So I conducted a brief survey with just over a thousand Christian women (white, non-white, cisgender, trans women, able- and less able-bodied) aged from fourteen to twenty-four. They were asked to finish these three statements:

1. The kind of girl I'm not is . . .

2. The kind of girl I am is . . .

3. The kind of girl I want to be is . . .

I felt cautious about heading into this space.

Not because of what I would find, but because of what I was asking of these women. I also spent a lot of time wondering whether I should use the word 'girl' or 'person'. Culture has programmed the female person to objectify herself. To see herself as a project to be worked on rather than the glorious and maturing woman she already is. So I chose 'girl' in the knowledge that it would allow me to get under the skin of how girls and women feel about their femaleness.

I was struck by two themes in the responses. First was the way the respondents tended to 'other' the women they felt they were not. Responses to 'The kind of girl I'm not is . . .' were mostly the labels often used against girls, like 'Easy', 'Slut' and 'Shallow'. Were these girls revealing a judgemental streak towards other girls, or were they revealing their own fears that others may label *them* this way?

The other theme that stood out was in response to the last statement, 'The kind of girl I want to be is . . .', where one word appeared in over 90 per cent of the 1,000 responses: 'Confident'. One participant even wrote, 'To find my feet as a woman.'

Confident.

In a world of conflicting messages and sometimes aggressive social norms around gender, these women long to be certain that they're living out their calling as followers of Jesus. To be sure that God has chosen them, not *because* they're women, but *as* women. I felt so encouraged by this, but also compelled to respond, because I don't believe we're called to *abide* by gender stereotypes, but to *reshape* them in the light of who we know God to be and who he says we are. To be women who challenge injustice, offer hope and create culture.

Born into a specific cultural view of femaleness, but surrendered to God.

Christian female empowerment isn't power for power's sake or to get one over on the guys. It's not liberation so that we can be selfish and individualistic in the way we live. It's power for a purpose – to see God's kingdom come on earth as in heaven – and it's power under authority: God's authority. So being a powerful woman by definition will mean a whole range of different things depending on who you are. I asked some Christian women who lead in the church, politics, human rights, journalism and youth ministry to share what they believe being a powerful woman means.

'Being a powerful woman means feeling the fear of being a pioneer, yet being one anyway. It means choosing to break down barriers or smash glass ceilings even though it's been implied that you shouldn't or you can't. Being a powerful woman means surrounding yourself with women and men that build you up so that you can go forward and be who God has called you to be. Being a powerful woman means taking courage.'

Chine McDonald

'To know your worth, just by being you – created in God's image, knowing that you are loved, no matter what. A powerful woman has worked hard to have a great deal of self-respect, and the love and respect of others. She shows integrity, letting people know when something's not right, and daring to live a vulnerable life.'

Line Stordal

'Every time you choose to forgive, every time you reach out your hand to those in need, every time you act justly or love mercy, every time you choose to do the right thing out of love, every time you turn your fear, your pain or your disappointment into a battle cry of prayer or worship, every time you get back up again, every time you laugh, smile or shed a tear, every time you speak life, light, hope, truth, freedom into someone or something – you are demonstrating what it is to be a powerful woman.'

Sarah Lang

'Through Jesus I have become God's daughter. That means I am royalty with the highest mandate ever. I am loved, chosen and called to participate in building his kingdom. That is the highest power bestowed on me to give me privilege and mandate, love and a calling.'

Evi Roderman

'Being powerful is born out of total utter dependency on the author of my life: Jesus. Without him I am nothing, but in his hands, my weaknesses are overruled by his Spirit's anointing.'

Anne Calver

I know each one of these women well. Their words come with a deep trust in God and personal conviction that continues to be hard won. What strikes me as the common thread running through each of their unique perspectives is that being powerful is about being *called* by God, *equipped* in that calling, *engaged* in their context and *released* to serve and lead effectively.

1. Called woman

You have been called to God for a life of devotion to him. This is the same calling for everyone who takes up their cross and follows Christ. But you're also called for a specific purpose, and it can feel like a minefield trying to work out what that is! I have a little acronym – ABCD – that helps me to think about God's specific call on my life and to discern whether to pursue a certain career, job interview or opportunity. For example, does this job/training opportunity/career fit with what I know so far of my skills and abilities? Take a look at my ABCD and jot down your own responses.

Abilities. What do you naturally lean towards? Where do you feel most able to be yourself and live from your strengths? God placed Adam and Eve in Eden because it was brilliantly suitable for their flourishing. So do you know what the situations or roles are that you flourish in with all your God-given skills and abilities? Look for opportunities to stretch yourself and develop your resilience and confidence in what you can do.

Burden. Whose welfare or what issue do you carry in your heart? We tend to use the word 'burden' to express how we carry this – it's heavy. It's not orientated to our self-interest or success, and it can feel as if it's been *in* us for a while, even if we've only recently begun to recognise it.

Character. Who are you becoming? You have a unique way of relating to God, the world around you and other people that enables you to live out the call God has placed on your life. Ask yourself how you're investing in the development of your character – or do you shy away from challenges? Whether you're in the role you feel you should have or not, God will already be working on your character, so see every moment as a chance to grow to be more like Jesus.

Discovered. What experiences have you been through that have shaped you? Spend time reflecting on what you've learnt about God, yourself and others. Allowing yourself to process what you've been through, both the positive and the negative, will give you insights into situations and greater empathy with people you may not normally connect with. God will use these to serve his purposes through your life.

What surprises you from your responses to any of these areas? What do you feel has been reinforced that you already knew about yourself?

2. Equipped woman

When God calls us, he equips us. First we are anointed by the Holy Spirit in power and authority. We know, from Scripture and our own experience, that God can take anyone and empower them with all they need to obey his call.

The secret to being equipped is prayer. Nothing, absolutely nothing, is as significant to the effectiveness of a leader as their prayer life. Make it your priority to get to know God through getting into the Bible – you could begin by reading a chapter a day, choosing one verse and reading it through a few times as you ask God to speak to you

– and through conversations with Christians whose views you share, as well as those whose opinions or theology may differ from yours. I think we have to accept that, despite our best efforts to learn from the Bible and from others, we're not God and we'll never know everything – so it stands to reason that we may hold convictions about faith that aren't right or need developing. I want to encourage you to equip yourself with the humility to listen before you speak, and bring everything to God in prayer. My favourite opener with God at the moment is, 'I've done it again – acted as if I knew more about you than I do. Forgive me, Lord, and please speak to me. I'm listening.'

We also have the responsibility to make the most of the opportunities we're offered, or can take up, to develop our characters and minds well. If God is calling you into politics, then it makes sense to determine, through hard work and dedication, to be a really effective civil servant or politician. Be rigorous with your calling, get the qualifications you need so that once you're in the position God has for you, you will exercise your influence and power with more compassion and mindfulness for all those you lead.

3. Engaged woman

I love to see Christian women of all ages adopt an attitude of ready engagement in their context. This means paying attention to what's happening around you, so you can engage in exploring what's gone wrong and participating in the solutions. My friend Joanne popped up on Sky News recently, talking about the dangers of plastic waste to ocean life as well as the poorest people in the world. She spoke up and she spoke out, and in the weeks that followed, plastic waste became one of the leading stories of news feeds and radio stations. Another friend, Rachel, watched a documentary about children in the UK going hungry during the school holidays, and set up Make Lunch, a small charity that has a huge reach as it equips local churches to open their kitchens and halls and cook a hot meal every day for the children in their community. Then there's Anna, who volunteers at a local charity because she wants to be part of the solution to poverty in the city she's moved to for university.

These women, and many others, simply posed the question 'What can I do about what I see around me?' – and it led to all sorts of things. It's one thing to notice; it's quite another thing to be ready to be part of the response. I believe that Christians should be in all spheres of life, creating culture and transforming cultural stories. But we can't do it alone! Listen to the burden you carry, and when you can, lean in with your stance of ready engagement.

4. Released woman

Jesus' way of calling disciples was to draw them to orbit his life for a bit so he could train them and then release them to 'go and do greater things' in his name (John 14:12–14). But as well as being released into our calling, we have the opportunity to inspire and work on behalf of other women to step into their calling too.

Think about the women we hardly ever see on the platforms at our Christian events. Who are they? Older women? Young women? Women with disabilities? Women who suffer with poor mental or emotional health? Women who don't speak English well? Women who are not white? Women raising children alone? Women unable to have children? Single women? Women who carry scars? Women who are over a certain size? Women who don't come from a 'nice' area? How can we amplify each other's voices and serve each other's ministries so that the body of Christ is enriched and our world is reached with the good news of Jesus?

When I'm invited to speak at Christian festivals or conferences I now make a point of asking who are the other young women who have been invited. If I'm the only woman on an all-male line-up, I'll sometimes ask them to invite at least one more woman to attend. More recently I've turned down speaking events if they haven't asked any women of colour to speak. For too long I was the only young woman speaking at events. I counted it as an incredible honour to be trusted and invited, but I also believed that God was asking me to open up the way for many other women to speak. Not just because they were women, but because they were called and anointed by God.

Get over yourself!

Years ago I had a load of fun for a week serving on the speaking team at a large Christian festival in the UK. It wasn't until part way through that I noticed I was the only woman speaking on the main stage throughout the week. I was in my late twenties. The closer it got to 'my night', the more anxiety I felt as the increase in people around me telling me I was the 'only woman on the stage' reached fever pitch. Nobody was saying that I shouldn't speak, but the complete lack of other women on the platform was sowing a seed of doubt in my heart of whether I was 'allowed' to be there. I dreamt that I fell flat on my face and made a total idiot of myself. Do you ever have those 'It's as I get up on the stage that I discover I'm completely naked' dreams? Well, it was that times a hundred!

So I did the two things I knew I could do. First I prayed. 'God – I want to preach because I sense you're calling me to this. I only want to say what you'd have me say. So move me out of the way, Lord, if I'm barking up the wrong tree!' And then I subverted the platform. I had brought a power outfit with me to wear: sharp heels, 'take-me-seriously' trousers, 'don't-mess-with-me' top! I put them on ready for the evening meeting and looked in the mirror. *I look as if I'm wearing armour!* I thought. Then it dawned on me that if Jesus was inviting me to speak in his name, I didn't need to view the platform as a cage fight. I wasn't taking people on, I wasn't up for a fight. I was just being me, called and anointed by God.

So I scrabbled through my bag for my comfortable jeans, cowboy boots and a checked shirt. (Don't get distracted – it was in the early noughties and I felt good in it!) Later that evening, as I made my way across the huge stage to the lectern, I performed an almighty comedy fall, ending up lying flat on my face! I'll never forget the sharp intake of breath from everyone in the arena. I lay there thinking, *This has either worked or I'll never be invited back here again!* It helped that the theme for the evening was 'Change the atmosphere' and my opening line was 'It only takes one person in an arena of 7,000 to change the atmosphere!'

It did work – for me. I couldn't think of any other way of taking the toxicity of expectation out of the moment. I was one person. I was not speaking *for* women nor was I out to prove that women are as competent as men when it comes to speaking with authority. I was just me. Flawed but called. I have the utmost respect for the role of preaching and teaching, and a deep love for sharing the word of God with people, but it felt great to fall over, because when I stood up, I felt I could preach with freedom and authority what God had put in my heart.

More than anything, I had to let go of the limitations I was placing on myself due to my sex. I had to stop apologising for my gender getting in the way of what I felt God had called me to. I'm so grateful to the women and men who have inspired me on my journey. You and I are not 'just a woman' and we're absolutely not 'girls' any more. We're called to the adventure of serving and leading with men and with each other.

Power for resistance

Exercising our God-given power isn't only about what we take up, but also what we resist.

There's a story in Scripture of two women who choose to resist, even though it could cost them dearly. You find them in the book of Esther – but Esther isn't the only heroine of this story. In fact, we wouldn't properly be able to understand Esther's remarkable courage had this other woman not done what she did. Vashti, the first wife of King Ahasuerus, is the Persian princess who, like Esther, is incredibly beautiful, but unlike Esther loses her life for exercising her power.

Vashti and Esther never meet. By the time Esther appears Vashti has been removed but the scene has been set and we the readers realise with a sickening dread that this is a court and a king who is not safe for women. As we see Esther's predicament unfold, we see it only going one way – to her early death. Of course, we know the happy ending – but Esther doesn't. She only knows that the last woman who resisted the king was executed. But that doesn't stop her.

But back to Vashti. King Ahasuerus throws a lavish banquet in his palace to dazzle the rich and powerful of the world with his own immeasurable wealth and status. It lasts seven days and on the final day we're told that he has an idea for the grand finale – Vashti. Naked.

But Vashti is not a woman to be possessed by a man abusing his power. When the king's messengers arrive to take her to the banqueting hall, Vashti is ready with her response. No. And she's persistent. In fact, three times she sends back a message to her husband, inviting him to reconsider his inappropriate request. But he doesn't change his mind – and neither does she.

'Resistance to a tyrant is obedience to God.'

Elizabeth Staunton, writing in 1895[4]

There will be times in your life when you are in situations where you are no longer free to live out the call of God on your life. In these situations you are called to resist. To be a woman who says, 'Enough.' Even if that means you lose friends, your job or your position of influence.

If it is true that Vashti was executed as some scholars agree, then she never got to see Esther stand against the tyrant king and prevail. Could it be that Vashti's certainty in the rightness of her cause plagued the king and effected a change in his heart, making it possible for Esther to resist and be heard?

Maybe; maybe not. He was, after all, a vain man who only ever acted to protect his own self-interest.

But being powerful is *never* about the status or honour that other people shower you with. It's *not* about being part of the elite who make the rules. It's about living out the rightness of God's cause, whether you see the impact immediately – or never do. Don't wait for a change in your circumstance to engage and resist.

Start now!

De-construct me

We need to unpick in our own thinking the idea we receive from culture that overt female sexuality is the root of women's power. Our equal standing before God and each other doesn't mean we mimic the aggressive, predatory tactics we see in toxic masculinity. We're not equal so that we can do things like the lads. We're released to obey the will of the Father – even if that means not looking powerful in other people's eyes.

CULTURE SAYS BEING POWERFUL MEANS:	JESUS SAYS BEING POWERFUL MEANS:
Getting what I want when I want it.	Laying down my dreams for the sake of others.
Controlling men with my sexuality.	Being self-controlled in my sexuality.
Being like men.	Being myself.
Winning.	Raising others up alongside me.
Being strong.	Being strong with his authority.
Being wealthy.	Using wealth wisely.

Your sexuality and your femaleness are powerful, but what really *empowers* your life as a woman is the infilling of the Holy Spirit producing in you the fruits of his work in your life. These are love, joy, peace, patience, faithfulness, kindness, goodness, self-control (Galatians 5:22–23). These are not feminine or masculine traits; they are Spirit of God traits. They are what will make you strong and able to exercise your power as a woman.

Re-construct me

This is a bit of a fun exercise, but it really works!

What comes to your mind when you think about someone being powerful? How are they standing? What's the expression on their face? What are they doing with their arms? Out of interest, is the person you're picturing a woman or a man? I'd like you to imagine a woman who is called, equipped, engaged and released in her power. How is she standing? What expression does she have on her face?

Right. Now I'd like you to copy her. (If you're in public somewhere you might like to wait until you get somewhere private, or not!) Pick a position that demonstrates her power – put your hands on your hips or in the air, lift your chest up, chin up, stand with your feet hip-distance apart, get that steely look in your eye or a huge smile on your face. It doesn't matter what you do, it just needs to say 'powerful'. Once you've found your power pose, hold it for thirty seconds, or sixty seconds if you're feeling up to it. It will probably make you giggle – but persevere!

How do you feel now? It's amazing how the way we hold ourselves physically can have such a direct impact on how we feel about ourselves. I've never managed to do this without having a little laugh at myself. But that's OK! Don't take your power pose too seriously, but take the reality of your power as a woman of God seriously.

You are powerful. You are a called, equipped, engaged and released woman. The world is waiting for you.

II.

HEART

A while back there was a series on TV that sought to challenge the British aversion to nudity. Contestants got to choose to date someone on their physical attributes alone. The only part of their potential date's body the contestants *didn't* get to see was their face. The message was simple: Like the pecs? You might like the man. Like the boobs? You'll love getting to know this woman. But I'm not sure how focusing on the size of someone's physical attributes helps anyone discover the hidden depths of their character.

But as distasteful as shows like these are they none the less demonstrate something unknowingly redemptive. In the first episode we meet the fantastic Aina. Bright-eyed and clear-headed, here's a strong woman who's searching for a strong man. She's immediately drawn to the guy with the prosthetic leg. 'That tells a story,' she says as she begins to try to connect with this body as a person. At the end of the episode Aina chooses him and when they finally get to stand (still naked) in front of each other they stare into each other's eyes, hungry to make a connection with the *heart,* not just the body. It's their silent rebellion, their unconscious act of resistance because they bear the mark of a God who made us hungry for heart to heart connection.

Your heart is captivating.

Your heart is an ocean.

Wild, beautiful, mysterious. We're not machines to be programmed. We're humans to be explored and cherished. It's in our hearts that we experience this power to reveal or conceal who we truly are, which is why we are told to guard them well. To pay attention to the very core of who we are becoming – because the whole of our life flows from it.

'Guard your heart above all else,
for it determines the course of your life.'

Proverbs 4:23, NLT

Some translations of this verse use the word 'wellspring' to describe our hearts, meaning an abundant source of something. For Christians, that source is God himself. It is within our hearts that we choose life or death as we connect with or disconnect from him. The destiny of your heart is to be connected with this abundant life of God – and to experience the transformation of your heart as you exchange fear for freedom, shame for strength. Knowing God brings your heart to *life*.

There's a group of leaders I meet and pray with on a regular basis. I'm so grateful for their friendship. It's hard not to love women who will listen to your woes, speak prophetically into your life and drink wine late at night in a hot tub with you! One of our get-togethers was the night before my trip to Moldova where, among other things, I would be meeting young female leaders eager to change their nation. I had spent the day at work searching for something I could give to encourage each of these incredible Moldovan women. Finally I grabbed a box of left over badges from some youth leader event we'd run the previous year. If I'm honest I chose them because they were hot pink – please don't judge me!

As we began to pray my friend Hellie shared a picture she'd received from God of me placing a small item into each woman's hands. A badge maybe? *Phew – that's what I've got!* I thought. *We're good to go.* Hellie, of course, didn't know about the pink badges stashed in the boot of my car.

'It's got a word on it that sums up what God has already placed deep within their hearts. Your job is to call it out of them.' Hellie paused. 'The problem is, they don't believe this is for them personally. So you'll need to place it in their hands.'

We waited a while as together we asked God what that word was.

'Courage.'

When I got back to the car and opened the box, I saw, in all their hot pink brilliance, a hundred badges each with the word COURAGE emblazoned on them! I can't describe what it was like the next day to meet the women that these badges of blessing were destined for. I've never experienced anything like it – God was not only wanting to speak *into* their hearts; he was wanting to speak to them *about* their hearts.

What might God be wanting to say to you about *your* heart?

Strong heart

Our word 'courage' comes from the French word *cœur*, meaning 'heart'. To have courage is to know your heart and to listen to it. To have courage is to speak from your heart, whatever the cost. This is the inner strength that comes from your everyday acts of courage as you live from your heart.

Being courageous and being brave aren't the same thing. We say that people are brave when they do a bungee jump or eat bugs without any sign of fear. But someone is courageous when they look deep into something, feel their fear and do it anyway. Living wholeheartedly is a courageous thing to do, because it requires us to look deep into our hearts and deal with the good, the bad and the ugly that lurks there.

But we don't do this alone. The most courageous act is to invite God to look deep into our ego, our essential self, and, like an expert surgeon, cut out the disease of sin so that we may experience endless life. 'Search me, O God, and know my heart; test my thoughts. Point out anything you find in me that makes you sad, and lead me along the path of everlasting life' (Psalm 139:23–24, TLB). All too often my heart hides a selfishness that surfaces when I feel under attack or stress. When disobedience finds a home in my heart, I need someone to search me with loving kindness and the ability to break the power of sin over my life. I ask God to search my heart because most of the time the deep cries of my heart are a mystery to me. Like the apostle Paul, I baffle myself with the knots I get tangled up in. How can I have lived with myself for so long and still know myself so little? I'm so grateful that when it comes to the matters of my heart I'm not alone in searching for myself.

'I don't understand myself at all, for I really want to do what is right, but I can't. I do what I don't want to—what I hate. I know perfectly well that what I am doing is wrong, and my bad conscience proves that I agree with these laws I am breaking. But I can't help myself because I'm no longer doing it. It is sin inside me that is stronger than I am that makes me do these evil things.

I know I am rotten through and through so far as my old sinful nature is concerned. No matter which way I turn I can't make myself do right. I want to but I can't. When I want to do good, I don't; and when I try not to do wrong, I do it anyway. Now if I am doing what I don't want to, it is plain where the trouble is: sin still has me in its evil grasp.'

Romans 7:15–20, TLB

The thing about our hearts is that they do bear the marks and scars of what we go through. A friend who went through a bitter relationship break-up defined the pain she experienced as like someone reaching into her chest, grabbing her heart and slowly ripping it apart. Sometimes it can feel as though our hearts are damaged beyond repair. Distrust, bitterness, rage and contempt often flow from wounded hearts that have given up the hope of healing.

But I really believe that there is healing for wounded hearts. Peace for troubled hearts. Joy for despairing hearts. Love for cold hearts. What Jesus offers us is life for our dying hearts and the chance to live strong-hearted.

Did you ever pray 'The Prayer'? The one where you invite Jesus into your heart? I did, at a church holiday Bible club when I was eight years old. I still do, every day. But as I've got older I've come to see that what really happens is that Jesus invites me into his heart. Compared to God's heart mine is a teardrop falling into the Atlantic Ocean. My life expands as I fall into his. My heart changes as I take on his character. The more time I spend immersed in who Jesus is, the more I take on his heart and his ways.

Character comes from *caractère,* which means a stamping tool. So your character, that distinct combination of qualities, makes a mark on others. It's meant to. Your character is how the marks of your heart are revealed to the world. So what should those marks be? Here are six marks of a strong heart.

1. A loved heart

A strong heart is a loved heart.

God loves your heart with a fierce passion and protective zeal. The Old Testament prophets were eloquent on the strength of God's unquenchable love for his people.

"". . . Israel, out looking for a place to rest,
met God out looking for them!"
God told them, "I've never quit loving you and never will.
Expect love, love, and more love!
And so now I'll start over with you and build you up again . . .
You'll resume your singing,

grabbing tambourines and joining the dance . . ."'

Jeremiah 31:3–6, The Message

Knowing that your heart is loved by God is reason enough to pay attention to it and to cherish it.

Do you ever find yourself talking about how much you love your friend's heart? Or saying, 'So-and-so has an amazing heart'? I find I say it when I'm thinking about my friend's incredible capacity to love others. My friend Katy has a heart like this. She continually goes the extra twenty miles for people. I love this about her, and the times I see her kindness being exploited or taken for granted get me really mad. I want her to give and give and give but also be so wise about where she allows her heart to take her.

I wonder if this is how God feels about our hearts?

He knows what stirs our hearts and what wounds our hearts. He knows what feeds us and what stifles us. He delights in the things that fill our hearts with love, and he gives us more and more and more love! He loves us extravagantly – and amazingly he trusts our hearts with the job of sharing his love with others.

You are loved completely so that you can love completely. Make this one of the marks of your heart.

2. A tender heart

A strong heart is a tender heart.

> 'Be kind to one another, tender-hearted, forgiving one another, as God in Christ forgave you.'

Ephesians 4:32, ESV

Nothing hurts my heart as much as withholding forgiveness from someone. Unforgiveness may feel like a powerful weapon against the person who has hurt you. But it's like drinking poison and expecting the other person to die.

It's not easy to forgive. Whether it's a relatively small or an unthinkable thing, letting our heart forgive someone who has wronged us is a mighty act of trust and tenderness. It's trust that God is the judge of all hearts, and it's tenderness towards ourselves. We know that in forgiving us Jesus makes it possible for us to forgive ourselves and others. Forgiving someone leaves you tender, but not broken.

Something on the road to recovery is tender, the way a bruise on my body is tender. The memory of a previous hurt, even a forgiven hurt, can be tender. Choosing the mark of a tender heart is an acknowledgement that you have been hurt and yet have chosen forgiveness. It is also a mark that speaks of being safe for another hurting heart to be around. If I'm dealing with my own need to forgive and be forgiven, you can be safe in the knowledge that I won't load my unresolved issues onto your tender heart. A tender heart is a safe heart.

Forgive. Become whole. Be tender-hearted to yourself and towards others. Make this one of the marks of your heart.

3. A faithful heart

A strong heart is a faithful heart.

> 'Let love and faithfulness never leave you; bind them around your neck, write them on the tablet of your heart.'
> Proverbs 3:3, NIV

Three girls approached me at a youth festival. Proudly they showed me their right forearms, red and blotchy with identical cross tattoos. 'We got this done today!' one of them blurted out. 'We heard you last night, and decided to follow Jesus. We got tattoos to remind ourselves that we will never turn back from this decision.'

Wow.

They literally inked the promise of their hearts onto their bodies. Scripture asks us to go one level deeper. Not skin and flesh but heart and will. To etch your faithfulness to God on the walls of your heart; to press into the depths of your ego and psyche that you are for God. 'Place me like a seal on your heart, like a seal on your arm' (Song of Solomon 8:6, NCV).

Faithfulness to God shows up in our lives in so many ways. What are you like with your time and money? What are you like in your relationships, both romantic and non-romantic ones? Do you show more faithfulness to the idols of sex, money and power? Choosing faithfulness as a mark of our hearts is saying that we consider God to be the greatest treasure we could ever have. Where our treasure is our hearts are found. Let the treasure you seek with your heart be God alone. What you will find will not disappoint you.

Choose faithfulness. Let the prize that is Christ flood the longings of your heart. Make this one of the marks of your heart.

4. A pure heart

A strong heart is a pure heart.

> 'Create in me a pure heart, O God.'
>
> Psalm 51:10, NIV

Whenever we hear the word 'purity' our minds often jump to the things we do that are right or wrong. This is part of the story, but not all of it. Think of purity as the quality of something, how authentic it is. Like pure water which is water from a source that has removed all impurities, or pure air that doesn't contain any poisons. Dirty water or noxious air is no longer pure; it's contaminated and needs to be purified to be life-giving to us.

The same is true of our hearts. What happens deep in the core of our being matters to Jesus because it is out of the condition of our heart that our actions occur. We either obey God's commands because we're devoted to him in our hearts, or we follow our own ideas because we're devoted to ourselves in our hearts. To have a pure heart means committing ourselves totally to living a life that pleases God. 'How can a [woman] stay pure? By obeying your word' (Psalm 119:9, NLT). It means that in our hearts we are choosing to be devoted to listening to and obeying God's word, even if it is in conflict with how we might want to live. God asks me to forgive, not hold grudges. He asks me to be generous with what I have been given, not hoard it all for myself. He asks me to only be sexually intimate with the person I have made a cov-enant commitment with. These things are hard – and

I know in my own life, they get to the heart of who it is I believe I am living for: myself or God.

But the demands God makes of us carry a blessing too.

On the side of a mountain Jesus preached what would later be referred to as the 'Sermon on the Mount'. In it he spoke of the pure in heart seeing God (Matthew 5:8). Not only is this a promise that as we devote ourselves to him God will reveal himself to us, but it's also an insight into the power of commitment to allow us to see what truly matters.

Years ago I took my friend Dave to an all-boys school to talk about the importance of trust, respect and commitment in intimate relationships. Dave began to tell these sixth-form lads about his obsession with porn as a teenager, and how it messed up a few of his relationships. He talked about the shame he felt and how he knew he needed to change not only his online habits, but the desires in his heart to not want to be using women's bodies in this way. Over time he worked with a mentor to break the habits and compulsions he felt for viewing online porn. Then he got married and now his wife was pregnant. The boys had been listening with increasing interest to Dave's story. 'To be honest, when my wife got pregnant her body began to change. She got fatter and rounder, all the things an adolescence hooked on the kind of porn I was devouring told me to despise.' The boys jeered at the thought of a female body changing in this way. Once they were quiet again Dave spoke. 'But here's the truth, boys. She has never been more beautiful to me than she is now.'

Choosing to walk away from the porn he was filling his heart with meant that Dave was free to see the beauty and wonder of his wife as she was, not as porn told him women should be.

Jesus says that the pure in heart will see God, because pursuing purity enables us to see God for who he is and what he's done. Through the sacrifice of Jesus, God makes purity of devotion to him possible. So ask him to strengthen your devotion to him and to show you how you can live in ways that please him.

Chase purity. Dare to devote your heart fully to God. Make this one of the marks of your heart.

5. A peaceful heart

A strong heart is a peaceful heart.

> 'Those who go to God Most High for safety
> will be protected by the Almighty.
> I will say to the LORD, "You are my place of safety
> and protection.
> You are my God and I trust you."'
>
> Psalm 91:1–2, NCV

My husband and I went for a walk around a lake one wild autumn day. Moaning because I was in wet-weather gear (I know it's good but how I hate it!) and wishing for a coffee shop around the next corner, I wasn't aware that the weather had changed and a storm was gathering speed around us. As we turned a corner the wind picked me up and threw me onto the ground. My husband managed to grab me and drag me behind the shelter of a tree. 'You so deserved that, Rach,' Jason laughed. 'You've been such a nightmare for the whole walk!' I wasn't hurt – apart from my pride! But to prevent it happening again we sheltered by the tree for a bit. No one else came by. Who else in their right mind would be out in this? But even in the eye of the storm, we had found a place of peace and calm. It was amazing.

A heart at peace is a heart that is learning to trust that God is always with us. One of the best explanations I can think of for trust is that ability to stretch out your arms and allow yourself to be held by God. This is so much easier to say than to do, especially as we can't literally lean back and be caught by God! But you can give up the wrestle in your heart to find your own peace, and invite the Spirit to give you his peace. Simply ask him, and then wait in stillness for his peace to come.

The storms of life might be all around you, but as you wait to receive God's peace, you'll know peace at the very core of your being. This storm will pass, and there is a journey to keep heading out on.

Ask for peace. God has all the power and he shelters you. Whatever comes your way, you are held and loved. Make this one of the marks of your heart.

6. A wild heart

A strong heart is a wild heart.

'We have freedom now, because Christ made us free. So stand strong. Do not change and go back into the slavery of the law.'

Galatians 5:1, NCV

What's the landscape of your heart? I reject the idea that women's hearts are basically indoor spas whereas men's hearts are wild terrain. We are wild at heart! Being a wild woman may come with all sorts of connotations of sense-less abandon. But that's being out of control and not knowing how to care for yourself. Wildness is different. Think about animals out in the wilds of the Australian outback or the African plains. They know their environment, where to get food, how to survive a crisis, who to run in a pack with. They can detect danger from afar and because of their natural instinct towards freedom, will do what it takes to be free and stay free.

This is your heart too.

You are born with an instinct for freedom. When your heart is God's, your heart is free.

When your heart has been brought to life by the Spirit, it is no longer controlled or imprisoned. 'So Christ has made us free. Now make sure that you stay free, and don't get all tied up again in the chains of slavery' (Galatians 5:1, TLB). Paul is making it clear that the power to remain free is within our hearts. It *is* also possible for us to be wrapped up in chains again.

Where there are signs of slavery to the belief that we need to work for our salvation, as if Jesus' sacrifice isn't enough for us, it's a sign that we've lost sight of who we are – free women, at the expense of all Christ has won for us. We may have been raised by women who carry the legacy of slavery to fear and shame – and they've passed it on. But this can end with you. Jesus breaks the legacy of fear over your life. Simply ask him. Find a friend to stand with you as you embrace your freedom and lean into your wildness!

Be free. Let him release your heart so that you can run into all he has won for you. Make this one of the marks of your heart.

Powerful pants

Sometimes I take myself off on mini retreats to ask God to search my heart and re-envison my life.

One time I managed to get out of my front door before realising I'd not packed any clean knickers. So I ran back inside and grabbed the first pair that were drying on the radiator. Yikes. Big Spanx pants! What were they doing there? But I didn't have time to go hunting for normal knickers, so off I went. The next day I found myself wandering round a little park near to the hotel I was staying in, wearing scruffy jeans, battered old trainers but the strongest pants in the world – I felt amazing.

God isn't Spanx!

He's something far better. Because in the hidden place of your innermost self, God is grounding you in his love and transforming you with his mercy and grace. This glorious inner strength of the Spirit at work in your heart is making things happen.

'I ask him to strengthen you by his Spirit – not a brute strength but a glorious inner strength – that Christ will live in you as you open the door and invite him in. And I ask him that with both feet planted firmly on love, you'll be able to take in with all followers of Jesus the extravagant dimensions of Christ's love. Reach out and experience the breadth! Test its length! Plumb the depths! Rise to the heights! Live full lives, full in the fullness of God. God can do anything, you know – far more than you could ever imagine or guess or request in your wildest dreams! He does it not by pushing us around but by working within us, his Spirit deeply and gently within us.'

Ephesians 3:16–20, *The Message*

De-construct me

I invite you to simply allow God to speak to you about the condition of your heart. I find that God often uses the landscape around us to provoke and give us insights into the landscape of our hearts, so why not get outside if you can, and walk and talk with God about any de-construction of false beliefs or damaging behaviours that needs to happen for your heart to be whole and strong. A great prayer is this: 'Lord, may what I see around me give me some insight into what you see inside me.'

You might find that God brings to your mind things you know you need to be free of. Repentance is a word that speaks of an ultimate, unconditional surrender to Jesus. As we speak out the things we've thought or done that we know have dishonoured God, ourselves or others, we can know forgiveness and the chance to choose to live from our hearts in ways that put God first.

You could use these three Rs to help you:

Reject – what are some of the unhelpful attitudes in culture around you that you're tempted to believe, but know aren't life-bringing for your heart?

Renounce – what have you been depending on to comfort or satisfy your heart instead of reaching out for God?

Restore – invite Jesus to bring back or give you for the first time the peace, trust or purity that your heart longs for.

Re-construct me

If you can, pick one of the six 'marks of the heart' from this chapter (loved, tender, faithful, pure, peaceful, wild) that you feel is pertinent to your heart at the moment. I'm a fan of surrounding myself with little messages that remind me of the direction I want to grow in, so why not stick up around your bedroom or on the back of the toilet door 'I am tender-hearted' or whichever you've chosen? Then you need to define a few steps to help you move towards your goal. So as well as naming what you want your heart to be, identify two or three steps to help you reach it. Here's an example to get you started:

'I am wild-hearted.'

1. I won't ignore the random ideas for my life that pop into my head. They're worth catching and praying over.

2. When a fearful thought about a decision I've made or a hope I have drops into my head, I'll invite Jesus to weigh in with his love so that I don't pull back from something that could bring me and others so much life and joy.

3. I will do at least one thing a week for the next month that feels a bit out of my comfort zone!

12.

DIE

I adored my grandpa. He was a bit of an all-action hero in his youth – driving a lorry in a treacherous tank convoy across the African plains in the Second World War and later a motorbike as a dispatch rider. I have a black and white photo of him with his sleeves rolled up and no helmet on, grinning as he sets out on another adventure. In later years he smoked a pipe and taught us grandkids the secrets of the great outdoors as we chased him over the flint hills in north-west Kent where he lived.

The last time I saw him he had come out of his front door, as he always did, to wave me goodbye. He had his arm around Peggy, whom he had married later in life. He looked so content and full of life, even though I knew he was in pain. A week later he died.

His death felt so strange. At his cremation service I couldn't quite believe that my tall grandpa, so youthful for his ninety-odd years, was in a box, waiting to be swallowed up in the flames. My dad whispered, 'He's not here. In my imagination I can see him being fifteen years old again and running for all his worth over the hills.' As Grandpa loved Jesus I knew that one day I would see him again – but that didn't stop me grieving.

Being separated from our loved ones feel so wrong. It's

no wonder we grieve their passing because death *is* wrong! God never planned for physical death to be part of the journey of our lives. The gut-wrenching pain of being separated from the people we love is a sadness our hearts were never meant to bear. God created humanity to know *ongoing* existence in his presence, a reality that would know no interruption or loss. The universe that was made at God's command cannot function without working according to God's will. Sin, which is essentially a rejection of God's will, works against God, works against life itself and so introduces a shelf-life to existence that God never planned. It's like unplugging a mobile phone from its charger; it will keep going for a while, but in the end it'll switch off because it can't keep going indefinitely without being plugged into a power source.

We were made to be forever plugged in to the power source that is God. Author, English professor and all-round genius C.S. Lewis put it this way:

'Once a [wo]man is united to God, how could he not live forever? Once a [wo]man is separated from God, what can he do but wither and die?'[1]

But physical death *is* a reality for all of us. It's the one certainty in life. I wonder then why we find it so hard to talk about it in our society. Maybe because we realise that death marks an end to life as we know it, and we don't really know how to handle that, or what's on the other side. I have friends who believe that after death there is nothing, a total blank. It's the only logical view in a secular culture that has done away with the existence of

God. But even as they say they believe there is nothing after death their words ring hollow. Something inside them craves eternity. There's a cry in our world today that demands, 'There must be more than this!'

And we as Christians echo that heart cry for more life because we know that there *is* more, so much more. But in order to get it, we have to die first. Christianity celebrates death before it embraces life!

Death

I know that sounds strange, but when we choose to follow Jesus we're agreeing to lose our lives – to die to ourselves. Surrendering to Jesus means that we die to our way of doing things. We agree to give him every right and authority over who we are and how we will live. No matter what has gone before and who we might have been, from the moment we turn to Jesus a new life begins. 'This means that anyone who belongs to Christ has become a new person. The old life is gone; a new life has begun' (2 Corinthians 5:17, NLT). This is what we call the cost of following Jesus – it's the great exchange: everything we are, everything we have, everything we ever hope to be, all surrendered to Jesus for all that he is and making way for his designs, ambitions and hopes for us.

My friend knows this great exchange. She became a Christian after years of drug abuse. Every day she is learning to trust God more as she lets go of the ways she used to think and behave. When she's worshipping Jesus she has both arms stretched up high into the air, palms facing upwards. If you were to ask her why she does this she'd tell you that when you're in the presence of someone so much more powerful than you, all you can do is hold your hands up in surrender.

Jesus tells us, like he told his first disciples, that if we want to follow him the cost is our *total* surrender. It's the ultimate de-construction of who we are in the way the world defines us: our status, popularity, identity and even our understanding of God fall in a heap at Jesus' feet. This is because nothing we can achieve for ourselves is worth anything compared to who we are and who we can be in the hands of God. Even the best life we could give ourselves is like being given a candle when someone else is offering us the sun. Look at how Jesus puts it:

'If anyone wants to be a follower of mine, let [her] deny [her]self and take up [her] cross and follow me. For anyone who keeps [her] life for [her]self shall lose it; and anyone who loses [her] life for me shall find it again. What profit is there if you gain the whole world—and lose eternal life? What can be compared with the value of eternal life?'

(Matthew 16:24–26, TLB.)

Jesus knows that following him is the only path to the everlasting life we were made to know. So he's not afraid to invite us to die to everything else.

As we follow Jesus, we begin to die to being the one in the driving seat of our lives. We die:

. . . to knowing all the answers.

. . . to expecting life to always be fair.

. . . to God always doing and being what we think he should.

. . . to being the one in charge.

. . . to having our voice heard and our opinion prioritised.

. . . to knowing for certain what's going to happen.

. . . to being successful, wealthy, popular or significant in the eyes of the world.

These small deaths are painful – some aren't small at all. Our egos don't want to hand over the reins of our lives, so we find we're in a battle with our own selves as we try to relinquish control. Although I want to surrender to Jesus, I don't like accepting that there may be some things Jesus will ask of me that won't win me likes on social media or success in my career or security in knowing I'll always live somewhere with great health care and low crime rates!

But I know that without dying to myself, I cannot truly follow Jesus. So I have to ask myself: if these deaths are not happening in my life, is it Jesus I'm following, or some version of him I've invented? A Jesus who never challenges my self-centredness or invades my comfort with the call to risk everything for him is not the Jesus who suffered and died so that I could know life in all its fullness. The Jesus in Scripture who asks me to follow him says some hard things about what will happen to me as I surrender to him. But worse, he says some even harder things about what it means if I don't. 'If you refuse to take up your cross and follow me, you are not worthy of being mine. If you cling to your life, you will lose it; but if you give up your life for me, you will find it' (Matthew 10:38–39, NLT).

It's strange to think that when Jesus said these words, he hadn't been crucified or raised back to life. As far as the first disciples were concerned, carrying your cross was part of the torture their hated enemies the Romans inflicted on criminals who were about to be executed on that same cross. When Jesus told his closest friends that loving him meant surrendering to the cruellest death at the hands of their oppressors, what might they have thought? I can imagine them muttering to themselves, 'Jesus, are you saying that following you means we will end up dead? What does carrying a cross have to do with following you?' Later, when they saw Jesus carrying his own cross up a hill to his death, these words must have come back to them with a new significance.

You have a cross to carry. So do I. Some people think it's a symbol of the annoying person at work that they have to deal with, or an illness they need to bear. But for the first disciples the cross was painfully literal – it meant being willing to suffer and even die in the name of the one you're following. Dietrich Bonhoeffer, a German pastor and theologian who was ultimately executed for his part in a failed plot to assassinate Adolf Hitler, said this about carrying our cross:

'The cross is laid on every Christian. The first Christ-suffering which every man must experience is the call to abandon the attachments of this world. It is that dying of the old man which is the result of his encounter with Christ. As we embark upon discipleship we surrender ourselves to Christ in union with his death – we give over our lives to death. Thus it begins; the cross is not the terrible end to an otherwise god-fearing and happy life, but it meets us at the beginning of our communion with Christ. When Christ calls a man, he bids him come and die.'

Dietrich Bonhoeffer, *The Cost of Discipleship*[2]

Bonhoeffer is right – what our society often sees as an end, Jesus sees as *the* new beginning. It's the seed falling to the ground and splitting open so that new shoots can grow. It's the wheat being crushed to make bread. It's the bread being broken to feed many. It's life being given away in the service of others.

This is what the surrendered life looks like in practice – to see ourselves as serving the people around us. After a heated exchange with his disciples where James and John ask Jesus if they can sit alongside him in the new kingdom, Jesus gives us a stunning insight into the life he came to lead, and the life he expects us to imitate. 'This is what the Son of Man has done,' Jesus tells them. 'He came to serve, not to be served—and then to give away his life in exchange for many who are held hostage' (Mark 10:45, *The Message*).

Don't be fooled by the idea that being a servant means popping in to clean the house a few hours a week. A better translation of the Greek word *doulos*, which Mark has Jesus use in the surrounding discussion of what it means to serve, is 'slave'. A servant has a contract and is paid for their services. A slave is owned, and the only identity they have is because of who they are owned by.

This destroys any idea we have that surrender to Jesus is a personal and private thing that we can share with people when we feel they're ready to hear about it. There's nothing private about being a slave and that's who you and I are – slaves to Christ.

It might seem odd, after reading a book that has been all about exploring everything God made you to be, that we should end here, in slavery. In today's struggle around female empowerment it sounds dangerous to ask women to die to themselves. Surely the church should be encouraging girls and women to *love* themselves, not *lose* themselves? Haven't we had enough of women being invisible in the church, written out of world history and being told to shut up, sit down or not to make a fuss? Isn't it time for us to take up our places as women anointed by God to love and lead, not relinquish our hard-won opportunities to show up and be seen? Isn't the suggestion that we die to ourselves just a glorified way of replacing one form of enslaving women with another?

Maybe . . . if it were anyone other than Jesus who was inviting us to walk this path.

The one who extends this invitation to us comes to us as a slave. He stoops down to wash our feet and we see in his hands the holes where the nails hung him to the cross to die. It's in these hands that he holds the power to give us life now, and for all eternity. There is no one else we should lose ourselves to. There is no one else who has the right to ask this of us. There is no one else we would ever dream of becoming 'enslaved' to.

This is where the true wonder and wildness kicks in. All throughout this book I've been inviting you to wake up to your precious life, to grab it with both hands, to know yourself intimately, to lead yourself in love and into love, and to reach out to the world around you with compassionate confidence and radiant power. This would be a great end in itself and if you walked away from this book knowing a little bit more of your worth and potential I would be so happy.

But there's more.

I don't just want to help you do a better job at becoming the best version of yourself. I think you're probably doing a brilliant job at that and you just need to believe in yourself a bit more.

No, what I really long for you is that you know with a deep conviction and joy that your life is *yours to give away*. That it is within your power to surrender it all to Jesus. And as you do, to know the utter abandonment and freedom that comes from being a woman who is fully surrendered and thoroughly alive to Christ.

Let me say it again – you can only give away what belonged to you in the first place. You can only choose to die to Christ if you know that you're alive to yourself to make that choice.

Life

When I started out as a naïve young youth worker I took a job as a support worker in a home for homeless young people with damaging addictive behaviours. I loved my work and I loved the young people. Many of them had experienced pain and abuse at the hands of relatives and friends, and years of numbing the pain with whatever they could lay their hands on had left them exhausted and ready to give up.

One night one of the young women gave up. She overdosed and ended up spending three days in hospital. I went to pick her up and bring her back to the hostel. It was a beautiful day, so we took a detour to a spot of outstanding natural beauty. It's a cliff that overlooks the English Channel. It's also a place with a reputation for people jumping to their death. I can't think what got into me to bring this young woman to the top of this cliff!

But I did.

I parked the car and we walked over the grass to the top of the cliff edge. The view was spectacular. A haze was rising off the sea and birds soared gently on the warm air.

For a while we sat on the grass near the edge, just taking in the view. I remember a bus load of tourists trundling by. No one really bothered with us: me and this young woman who was not dead, but not really alive. She finished her cigarette and asked, 'We going back yet?'

'No, not yet,' I replied. 'I think there's something we need to do first.'

'What?'

'I'll show you,' I said as I stood up and shuffled a little closer to the edge of the cliff.

'I'm alive,' I said. 'I'm alive. I'm alive.'

'You're weird,' she muttered, reaching for another cigarette.

'I know. But come and join me.'

She gave me a long look. Then got up and stood next to me. Quietly at first, but then with more determination, she joined me in shouting out to the gulls and the clouds, 'I am alive!'

You have been given your own life to live as you choose. This is your free will. It's both a beautiful and a terrifying thing to be alive. But in his grace and mercy, Jesus offers us the chance to hand it all over to him, and in that surrender to know him in greater and greater measure. Because we've been raised on individualism we find it hard to believe that the best life comes through surrender. But it does. This is what I crave more than anything: to know Jesus more and more. So that the older I get, the more surrendered I am. It's my dream that the gods of my false self that I'm struggling to put to death today present less of challenge for me to surrender tomorrow.

The call in the Gospels (and it's repeated many times) is to die to self and to outdo each other in how much of yourself you give away in love. This is one of the secrets of dying to self – it should be done in love. It's the greatest motivator.

I've heard of a park somewhere in Europe that has a very beautiful flower bed with a sign written in three languages. In German it says, 'Picking flowers is prohibited.' In English it says, 'We ask you not to pick the flowers.' In French it says, 'Those who love flowers will not pick them.'

Who knows if it's true? But it brilliantly reveals the three great motivators of fear (if you pick the flowers you'll be breaking the law), approval (we'll like you more if you don't pick the flowers) and love (if you really love flowers, you wouldn't want to ruin this flower bed). Each approach at preventing people from picking the flowers might serve the same outcome, but only one is actually about the real issue. If you love the flowers enough, you won't need telling not to pick them!

What's the best way to motivate you? It's probably a combination of all three. Society functions on the fact that most of the time most of the population don't want to break the law and have to deal with the consequences. Most of us quite like keeping people happy so don't mind

obliging people's requests if it makes life better for
ourselves in the long run. Then there's love. I don't pick
up my little daughter from school because I'm afraid of
the local authority being informed I'm a bad parent, or
because I want to keep on her good side. I pick her up
from school because I love her.

I also pick her up from school because it's become a
habit, a rhythm of my life. I shape the rest of my day
around this event. I've walked away from job opportunities or missed out on meeting my hero (I'll tell you that
story another time) because I needed to get home to do
the school run. OK, so I'm labouring the point. But the
point is that being motivated by love can often feel like
you're being controlled by routine, duty, practice. But it's
a practice I completely buy in to.

The same applies to the cost of discipleship. Jesus could
have said, 'Deny yourself and follow me – that's an order!'
He didn't. He could have said, 'Please deny yourself and
follow me. The Father will like you so much more if you
do.' He didn't. Instead he appealed to our love for him:
'Anyone who wants to follow me must put aside his own
desires and conveniences and carry his cross with him
every day and *keep close to me*!' (Luke 9:23, TLB).

So you need to die in order to live; deny yourself in
order to find yourself; become a slave to find true freedom.
It's not surprising that for many people hearing this, Jesus'
way doesn't sound like the key to setting you truly free.
But in truth it's the *only* thing that will. Surrender is the
only path to real satisfaction.

When I was in my early twenties a friend (of the same
age) decided to become a nun. So she tripped off to a

convent for a couple of years to explore her vocation. For all she loved about it, she felt God call her out of convent life and explore a life of surrender to him but one not set apart from society. She'd only recently made the move when I invited her to come on holiday with me and a few mates to an isolated area of north Brittany. One friend, atheist Matt, was a bit dubious about having an ex-nun on the trip.

'You'll love her,' I coaxed. 'She won't make you do 4.00 a.m. matins or anything. Come along.'

'Make me do *what*?' he asked, sounding nervous.

Part way through the week we trundled down a little lane to one of those beaches that's wide and wild. Sand-dunes created little hideouts so we could shelter from the winds that were whipping in from the sea.

'I still don't understand your faith, Rachel,' Matt was saying. 'Isn't it frustrating to be told what to do and what to think? How can you be yourself when you're constantly told to deny yourself? It's not for me. I like being free.'

As he was speaking I could see my ex-nun friend crouching behind another dune to strip down to her knickers and bra. Standing up she smiled at me and then ran, laughing and whooping, across the wet sand and into the sea. Matt sat with his mouth wide open, watching her.

'What's she doing?' asked Matt, clearly a little impressed.

'Denying herself and loving being free!' I laughed.

Dying to Jesus opens up a life of freedom that is sweeter and wilder than we could ever dream of. My friend partied in the waves because even though she had no idea of the next steps, she knew she belonged completely and fully to the God who made her and had a plan for her life. She was ready to die any number of deaths to herself to gain all that she would find in Jesus.

This journey you're on of finding who you are begins here, at your point of surrender. I can walk with you up until this moment, but here is where I have to step back. Everyone and everything steps back – it's just you and Jesus. You wonder if you've got what it takes to die to yourself. Won't it be too difficult, too painful? Are you courageous enough? But being brave is simply finding that you have it in your heart to live courageously with your one wild life. And in a moment of raw courage, you say yes. Then you say it again. Over and over on a daily basis as your life finds freedom in surrendering to Jesus.

There's no way of knowing what lies around the corner. But as you turn into each new bend in the road, you can know that you're following Jesus. He's already there, waiting for you as you find your strength in laying down your life, and your purpose in picking up your cross. He will be with you from here and into all eternity.

De-construct

I once took a group of teenagers, none of whom were Christian, into an Anglo-Catholic church – because they wanted to try out praying. One girl looked at me in horror when she noticed: 'There's a man on the cross. Gross!' The cross is a popular symbol in our culture today, whether it's on jewellery (sometimes like a lucky charm), a tattoo or a flag (often abused by far right groups who want to claim a pure ethnicity and stir up hatred against people who don't look like them), but it's been largely disassociated from its call to radical surrender to Jesus. The fact that the brown-skinned Middle Eastern man who hung on the cross is a direct threat to consumerism and the power of hatred is conveniently ignored.

Of course, for Christians, wearing or having a cross in our home is *all* about the counter-cultural way of life we're choosing. A friend of mine wears a cross around her neck because she wants to 'wear her surrender' as a reminder that she belongs to Jesus now.

Give yourself some time to unpack how you are approaching the cross. What are you bringing to the cross that you don't want or are struggling to surrender?

If you can, find a cross and pop it in the middle of a room (or draw one on a piece of paper). On smaller pieces of paper, write down the individual things you are struggling to die to. Here are some ideas to help you think specifically for yourself. Write down:

The wish list that God has to fulfil in order for you to follow him.

The things you look to for your identity before you look to God.

Those things you don't want to admit to anyone else because you feel shame.

Your disappointments with God and with other Christians.

Anything you know God has asked of you, but you're resisting.

Once you've written these down, place them over the cross. There is no condemnation for you, because you belong to God through the death and resurrection of Jesus. But here is your opportunity to invite Jesus to help you in each of these areas, to die to yourself and to receive the great exchange of your life for his life.

I asked for strength that I might achieve;
He made me weak that I might obey.
I asked for health that I might do greater things;
I was given grace that I might do better things.
I asked for riches that I might be happy;
I was given poverty that I might be wise.
I asked for power that I might have the praise of men;
I was given weakness that I might feel the need of God.
I asked for all things that I might enjoy life;
I was given life that I might enjoy all things.
I received nothing that I asked for, all that I hoped for.
My prayer was answered, I was most blessed.

Attributed to an unknown Confederate soldier

Re-construct

I'm getting myself into the habit of asking each morning, 'How surrendered can I be to you today, Jesus?' It's the most dangerous prayer I think I've ever prayed – because Jesus has a habit of answering it. Sometimes I twin this with another challenging question: 'When will I say no to myself today?' It acknowledges the fact that my ego will want to battle against my desire to surrender my ideas and sense of self-importance to Jesus. Here are some ideas to help you build a rhythm of surrender into your life.

1. The mundane – Look through your plans for the day and ask Jesus to speak to you about how he wants to use you in your regular routine. When you get an impression of what that might be, commit yourself to doing it. The more you can do this the easier daily surrender will become.

2. Mind the gap – As you go about your day, be ready for ways that Jesus might be wanting to use you in serving the people you bump into or the situations you find yourself in. When you sense he's asking you to go out of your way to serve someone, or lay down a plan or dream that you had, do it. It will build deep within you the experience of letting go and then leaning hard on God as you trust him for the outcome.

3. Embrace the freedom – Take in the moments when you discover a little bit more of the freedom that comes as you die to yourself. Make a note of these moments so that you can read back over them and remind yourself of what it's like to be choosing God's way, not yours.

4. Go hard after God – Sometimes Jesus asks us to pick up something and run with it. It might be a person he wants to reach through you, or an injustice he is asking you to call out. But as you build self-denial into your life, be open to embracing the mission God invites you to be a part of.

+.

RE-CONSTRUCT

I've tried to picture you as I've written this book.

I wonder if you've grabbed moments when you're on the bus or at your favourite coffee shop to flick through and land on pages you've liked. I hope my words have opened up a space inside you to find yourself as God sees you.

It's easy to see all the things we want to change about ourselves and others. It takes a woman who dares to be courageous with her life to shake off what needs to be left so that she can move forward lighter, stronger, more hopeful into all that's ahead of her. She's a woman who believes that the life she was made to live is found as she surrenders, and she also knows it will only be fully lived out in the age to come, when all things are made new.

I watched a woman destroy her life once.

She gathered up into one warehouse all the things she owned. Bike, clothing, rings, books, laptop, photos, phone, chairs, packet of tampons – everything! Then she borrowed a huge crushing machine, loaded all her possessions onto the conveyor belt, pressed the button and sat back to watch all her stuff get shredded. I, along with other curious bystanders, spent an afternoon with her watching her possessions turn to dust. It was one of the oddest things I've ever witnessed. I didn't feel sad, or regretful, or even impressed. I just felt her relief that once this was done, she would be free to walk away and rebuild her life in the way she wanted to.

Imagine if you could put on a conveyor belt all the things you know hurt your body, trap your mind, clutter up your soul and make you feel weak. What might it feel like to watch them be reduced to nothing but dust? Then Jesus, who has been loading stuff onto the belt with you, grabs your hand and pulls you towards the door, laughing, 'Come on, let's get out of here. There's so much I want to show you!'

Some of the people who came to the warehouse to watch are cheering you on! They've had their conveyor belt moment. They know what this means. Others are not liking how you've crushed the things that still mean so much to them, like status, success, perfection, wealth and being the boss of your life. They're not even sure you're right to step into the life of surrender, leadership, adventure and risk that you're running towards.

But that's OK.

Your job is to live as Jesus lives.

To dismantle anything that would prevent you receiving into your whole being and then living out the life that he offers. Because he *is* offering this life to you.

This is what I find so moving in the story of Jesus at the home of his friends Mary and Martha. They're women in a world where their identity is both precarious and limited. But Jesus invites them to be *disciples* in his Father's kingdom, where their new identity means everything.

'As Jesus and the disciples continued on their way to Jerusalem they came to a village where a woman named Martha welcomed them into her home. Her sister Mary sat on the floor, listening to Jesus as he talked.

But Martha was the jittery type and was worrying over the big dinner she was preparing.

She came to Jesus and said, "Sir, doesn't it seem unfair to you that my sister just sits here while I do all the work? Tell her to come and help me." But the Lord said to her, "Martha, dear friend, you are so upset over all these details! There is really only one thing worth being concerned about. Mary has discovered it—and I won't take it away from her!"'

Luke 10:38–42, TLB

Jesus doesn't tell Martha off for wanting to serve him a great meal. It is an act of great love that honours Jesus in the way that many other hosts forget to do. Remember Jesus reminding Simon that his hospitality was seriously lacking! Well, Martha's hospitality is outstanding. It's a total credit to her, and Jesus isn't for a moment diminishing that. But he's the God of the *more than*. He wants more in his relationship with Martha than for her to feed him. He wants to feed her – not flatbreads and roast lamb, but life itself. Jesus is asking Martha how much she is prepared to lay down, to sit at his feet and be his disciple.

I'm going to give the final words to Catherine of Siena (1347–80), a nun who lived in Rome. During a powerful encounter with the Spirit she heard Jesus asking her to leave her withdrawn life and enter the world again where she could be seen and her voice could be heard. She obeyed, and her words and witness touch lives still today.

As you find your feet as a woman who is loved, called and empowered by God, your life will send a light out that the darkness will never extinguish.

'Be who God meant you to be and you will set the world on fire.'

Catherine of Siena

Re-construct me

Throughout this book you've been invited to pause and think about what it is that makes you *you*, and what it is that has been stopping you from expanding into the woman God has made you to be. That simple action of pausing contains a huge amount of courage and I trust you've known the presence of Jesus with every new paragraph and page turn.

I wasn't sure how to end our journey of de-construction and re-construction. In my mind I picture the process of becoming who we are as less like finding an arrow in a car park that we follow to get us to the exit, and more like being on a beach with our bucket and spade and digging in the sand a new channel to the sea. Have you ever done that? There's a moment when the little channel you're digging in the sand meets the incoming wave, and the water that's backed up behind you rushes out into the vast expanse of the sea.

Freedom!

You're created to grow into the woman God made you to be. There are no limits to the depth of your character or the call on your life or the extent of your adventure as you devote yourself to growing into God, and thereby into yourself.

So here's the final exercise. I hope you're ready, because it's by far the best one.

Close this book, pick up your bucket and spade, and explore for yourself the life as a wild and wonderful woman that is out there waiting for you.

I'm cheering you on.

Rachel x

References

2. Desire

1. Anaïs Nin, *Nearer the Moon* (London: Peter Owen, 1966).
2. St Augustine of Hippo, *Letters*, 243:10.
3. Sarah Coakley, *God, Sexuality and the Self* (Cambridge: Cambridge University Press, 2013), p. 10.
4. Michael Le Page, 'Orgasms: a real "turn-off" for women', *New Scientist*, 20 June 2005. Accessed online: https://www.newscientist.com/article/dn7548-orgasms-a-real-turn-off-for-women/
5. Quoted in Janet Hodgson, *Making the Sign of the Cross* (Norwich: Canterbury Press, 2010), p. 34.

3. Close

1. Bryan Stevenson, 2014 Kastenmeier Lecture, University of Wisconsin Law School.
2. Gladys Aylward with Christine Hunter, *Gladys Aylward: The Little Woman* (Chicago: Moody, 1970).

4. Fear

1. N.T. Wright, *Following Jesus* (London: SPCK, 1994), pp. 55–56.
2. Gary Chapman, *The 5 Love Languages* (Chicago: Moody, 1992).

5. Perfection

1. Elias Aboujaoude, *Virtually You: The Dangerous Powers of the E-Personality* (New York: W. W. Norton, 2011), quoted in a lecture by Gareth Cheeseman, ACETUK, 2017.
2. Timothy Keller, *Making Sense of God* (London: Hodder & Stoughton, 2016), p. 87.

6. Mystery

1. Prayer of St Brendan via https://www.catholiccompany.com/getfed/prayer-st-brendan-the-voyager

7. Pause

1. Paul Kingsnorth, 'The end of solitude: in a hyperconnected world, are we losing the art of being alone?' *New Statesman*, 26 April 2017. Accessed online: https://www.newstatesman.com/2017/04/end-solitude-hyperconnected-world-are-we- losing-art-being-alone
2. Heather Saul, 'Young, successful, busy yet lonely: a generation empowered by the internet and plagued by loneliness', *The Independent*, 23 November 2016. Accessed online: https://

www.independent.co.uk/life-style/health-and-families/huggle-app-millennials-loneliness-a7434111.html

3. Brian Draper, *Soulfulness* (London: Hodder & Stoughton, 2016), pp. 67–68.

8. Hurt

1. Emili Sandé, 'Hurts', *Long Live the Angels* (Virgin Records: 16 September 2016).

2. Martin Luther King, 'Suffering and Faith', *Christian Century* 77 (Chicago, IL: 27 April 1960), p. 510. Accessed online: http://kingencyclopedia.stanford.edu/encyclopedia/documentsentry/suffering_and_faith/index.html

3. Brian Draper, *Soulfulness* (London: Hodder & Stoughton, 2016), p. 97.

4. Bryan Stevenson, 2014 Kastenmeier Lecture, University of Wisconsin Law School.

5. Jill Rowe, Tumblr. Accessed online: https://jillsrowe.tumblr.com/post/169168313933/may-you-know-goodness-and-grace-and-delight-and

9. Radiant

1. Russell T. Davies, 'The Parting of The Ways', *Doctor Who* (Cardiff: BBC, broadcast on BBC One, 18 June 2005).

2. Brené Brown, 'The Power of Vulnerability' (TEDxHouston, June 2010). Accessed online: https://www.ted.com/talks/brene_brown_on_vulnerability

3. See https://www.gottman.com/about/john-julie-gottman/

4. Marianne Williamson, *A Return to Love* (London: HarperCollins, 1992), p. 190.

10. Power

1. UNODC, Global Report on Trafficking in Persons 2016, pp. 7, 28. Accessed online: http://www.unodc.org/documents/data-and-analysis/glotip/2016_Global_Report_on_Trafficking_in_Persons.pdf
2. Dorothy L. Sayers, *Are Women Human?* (Grand Rapids, MI: Eerdmans, 1971), p. 68.
3. Beverly Campbell quoted in Heather Farrell, *Walking with the Women of the Old Testament*, (Springville, UT: Cedar Fort, 2017).
4. Elizabeth Staunton, *The Woman's Bible: A classic feminist perspective* (European Pub Co, 1895).

12. Die

1. C. S. Lewis, *Mere Christianity* (London: HarperCollins, 2012), p.176.
2. Dietrich Bonhoeffer, *The Cost of Discipleship* (New York: Touchstone, 1995), p. 89.

ACKNOWLEDGEMENTS

I did lots of leaning into lovely people while I was writing this book. They took my weight and helped me find what it was I was trying to say. I'm grateful. So my huge thanks go to

Katherine Venn, for helping me spot where to dig, then cheering me on,
Miriam's Munchies, for letting me make the table by the window my home,
Youthscape, for access to a photocopier and the sharpest of minds,
Brett Jordan, for being man enough to proofread a book for women,
The Peaches (Anne, Anne, Hellie and Miriam), for calling something new out of me,
Jason, for sharing this wide and wild life with me,
Daisy, for loving me to the moon and back.

HODDER &
STOUGHTON

Hodder & Stoughton is the UK's
leading Christian publisher,
with a wide range of books from
the bestselling authors in the UK
and around the world ranging from
Christian lifestyle and theology to
apologetics, testimony and fiction.
We also publish the world's
most popular Bible translation
in modern English, the New
International Version, renowned
for its accuracy and readability.